Monsters

Alison Croggon is an award-winning novelist, poet, theatre writer, critic, and editor. Born in South Africa, she has lived in the UK and is now based in Melbourne, Australia.

Monsters

a reckoning

ALISON CROGGON

SCRIBE
Melbourne • London

Scribe Publications
18–20 Edward St, Brunswick, Victoria 3056, Australia
2 John Street, Clerkenwell, London, WC1N 2ES, United Kingdom
3754 Pleasant Ave, Suite 100, Minneapolis, Minnesota 55409, USA

Published by Scribe 2021

Typeset in 12.25/16.5 pt Fournier MT by the publishers

Printed and bound in the UK by CPI Group (UK) Ltd, Croydon
CR0 4YY

Scribe is committed to the sustainable use of natural resources and
the use of paper products made responsibly from those resources.

978 1 950354 60 3 (US edition)
978 1 925713 39 8 (Australian edition)
978 1 913348 71 7 (UK edition)
978 1 925938 82 1 (ebook)

Catalogue records for this book are available from the National
Library of Australia and the British Library.

scribepublications.com
scribepublications.com.au
scribepublications.co.uk

But in order to deal with the untapped and dormant force of the previously subjugated, in order to survive as a human, moving, moral weight in the world, America and all the Western nations will be forced to re-examine themselves and release themselves from many things that are now taken to be sacred, and to discard nearly all the assumptions that have been used to justify their lives and their anguish and their crimes so long.

The Fire Next Time, James Baldwin

Whites, whether American or European, are addicted to delusion.

@annamericana, 3 October 2017

The curse

Unusually, I am alone in the house. Later, I think this is just as well. I don't want any witnesses to my indignity.

No, that's not true.

After I read her letter, I call my father. For once in my life, I permit myself to spill my guts open before him. I have never done this before, in all the conscious years of my five decades on this earth.

I howl down the phone. I display my fury, my spite, my desolation, my bitterness, my anguish. Let it be said. Let it all be said.

When I hang up, there's a momentary respite, as if an abscess has been lanced. But then it pounces, squeezing me in its intolerable grip.

I name it, for the first time.

It's pain. I can't do anything to stop it. I can numb it, or wait for it to go away.

I pour myself a whisky and listen to the weather pursuing its pathetic fallacy: the winter rain, hammering down on my tin roof in the heavy darkness.

It will never all be said.

'When one hears about another person's physical pain,' writes Elaine Scarry in her scrupulous masterpiece *The Body in Pain*, 'the events happening within the interior of that person's body may seem to have the remote character of some deep subterranean fact, belonging to an invisible geography that, however portentous, has no reality because it has not yet manifested itself on the visible surface of the earth.'

Pain's triumph is, she says, 'this absolute split between one's sense of one's own reality and the reality of other persons'. It is here, says Scarry, that language fails, in this space between what is undeniable for one person and unconfirmable for another. That other person may be so close that they are touching the one in pain, but they may as well be, in terms of their subjective being, inhabiting another galaxy.

Scarry examines the languages in which we attempt to describe physical pain: medical, religious, political, social. And she prises open, with her cool, intellectual scalpel, some of the darkest regions of human experience — in particular, the desire to inflict pain on another human being.

She makes a distinction between physical and emotional pain. Unlike physical pain, which has no meaning and no value, psychological suffering does have 'referential content', so much so that 'there is virtually no piece of literature that is *not* about suffering'. Physical pain, she argues, is asocial and preconscious, while psychological pain is part of the social experience of the mind. Many people have argued with the absoluteness of this distinction, on many grounds: linguistic, medical, experiential.

Right now, that distinction doesn't seem so absolute to me, either.

I am not expert in the worlds of physical pain. I hope I never will be. I have never been stoic. My experiences have all been temporary: minor accidents, migraines, illnesses, childbirth. Psychological pain? Emotional pain? They abide intimately in my body, in the smell that clings to my clothes and sheets, in the smoky oils in my hair, in my addictions, in the toxic narratives that I wind around myself, consciously and unconsciously, to protect myself.

Now all those narratives are torn open, and here, in the middle of the splintering, I no longer recognise my self. It's as if the self I have known, through myself, through others, is suddenly harshly illuminated from a new angle, all shadows fled. I see the histories that I have denied all my life, the wounds that I have ignored, the pain that I never acknowledged.

We speak of these things in metaphor. The heart, that smoothly muscled pump, can be pierced and torn; its valves can malfunction; its arteries or muscles can bulge and burst. It is an absurdity to say of this fleshly organ that it can break, as if it were made of bone or ice. But we all know what someone means when they say, *my heart is broken*.

My heart is broken. But now I understand that it always has been broken.

Once upon a time, I began another story with 'once upon a time'. I knew much less then than I do now. I was more hopeful, and more deluded, and almost certainly I had less compassion. Now I am more angry, less hopeful, and both more and less certain.

Even though I know that progress is a myth, I like to think I am a better person than I was — or at least, a more knowledgeable person. I am quite possibly exactly the same as I was twenty years ago, in the same way that a fountain, which is always spilling different water, is always the same fountain. Yet I am convinced that something has changed. It feels fundamental.

How does one measure change, especially in something as uncapturable as one's own self? Does a shift in perception count as change, in any case?

I think of the ageing Buster Keaton in Samuel Beckett's only movie, *Film*, an exploration of George Berkeley's pronouncement that 'to be is to be perceived'. Keaton, eighteen months from his own death, plays O, a man who is evading, more and more absurdly, the tyranny of being seen. But he is also escaping the tyranny of being: if to be is to be perceived, then not to be perceived is an extinction.

The camera's indifferent eye stalks O with his head hunched down, his hat over his eyes, flinching away from the gaze of others, as he hurries down a street, up a flight of stairs. At last he escapes to his room, where surely he will be safe. But no, a cat and a dog are looking at him. A parrot. A goldfish. A mirror. He evicts the cat and dog, covers the parrot cage and the goldfish bowl with his coat, conceals the mirror with a blanket. But still there are eyes: the buttons on a folder, the carved mask on the back of a chair, a picture on the wall that he tears down and rips up, trampling it into the ground. And all the time, the camera, which is never acknowledged, records everything for the unknown eyes that will watch it, fifty-two years later, on a computer screen.

Himself, finally, staring one-eyed into the camera with increasing horror, knowing that he can't escape his own perception of himself.

I always wanted to be invisible.

Once upon a time, there were three sisters. One was the oldest, one was the youngest, and the other was in the middle. They were born into histories, spoken and unspoken, that shaped the contours of their minds and their memories. And not one of those sisters escaped the curse.

There is no moral to be drawn from this fairytale. It isn't a story of redemption. Yet I know too that any story is a ghostly negative: all that is dark in the image is a record of light. And sometimes it's so hard to distinguish one shadow from another.

I can't even remember the final conversation I had with my sister. I had sent her flowers, because she was ill, because I was worried, because, despite everything, I am not a complete monster, and she called to thank me. I was touched. Perhaps the old non-conversation would finally be laid to rest, like the zombie that it is. Perhaps the fairytale of happy ever after would come true after all.

And then, in this tentative place, which might have been the beginning of a reconciliation, she started again on the same old, same old. I pleaded with her to stop; I told her that these things she was saying were not true, were none of my business, were nothing to do with me. But she went on and on and on.

Finally, I lost it. I remember shouting. I remember slamming the phone down — she called on the landline — and shaking for an hour afterwards.

A few months after that, she sent me the letter. Written as part of her therapy, it outlined all the ways in which I had abused her. It was her response to an email I'd written months before. My email was written with both despair and hope: despair at the accumulating toxicity between us; hope that perhaps if I addressed her accusations against me cleanly, clearly, unambiguously, she would understand who I actually am. Hope that perhaps we could both, finally, find a way to be honest with each other.

I was cautious with this email. I cc'd in both our parents, so she couldn't misrepresent what I said. I wanted above all to be clear, so I made sure that I made no counteraccusations: I confined myself solely to defending my character against the stories that she had been retailing to almost everyone we knew, both inside and outside the family, in some cases since we were young women.

I told her, for the first time in my life, how deeply these stories had hurt me.

'You are not a victim of me,' I wrote. 'You have never, ever been a victim of me. But you have said really horrible things about me. Just because you've been saying this stuff for years doesn't make it true. It just makes it worse. I have put up with this for years, being gracious for the sake of family harmony. I put up with it out of compassion for you, a compassion you have seldom extended to me. And after all these years, I don't see why I should put up with it any longer.'

Reading that now, I'm not surprised that it didn't end well. But when I wrote that email, I really did hope that we could repair our relationship, that perhaps we could become like siblings are supposed to be, when everything isn't broken. I see that sibling love — honest, clear-sighted, unconditional — between my children. I guess I wanted it for myself.

Perhaps the oddest thing is that I had never previously told her how much these stories wounded me. Perhaps it was because they seemed at once so trivial and absurdly incorrect that, aside from the odd argument, they scarcely seemed worth addressing. Perhaps I knew that she would simply deny that she had said any such thing, even if she had said it literally five minutes earlier. Perhaps — is this true? I am sure it is true — it was that I had always believed that addressing them would hurt *her*. That challenging those stories would wound her in a way that leaving them unchallenged wouldn't wound me.

She always placed me as a dark mother-figure, with a capacity for annihilation but not for feeling. Somehow, I had always believed that my resistance to pain was higher than hers, and that therefore it was incumbent on me to say nothing.

Her immediate answer to my email didn't address anything I had raised. Instead, there were new accusations. Later, in the final letter that broke us completely, there were more. I read that letter in growing rage because either she knew she was lying or she genuinely believed everything she was saying. I didn't know which, and I didn't know which was worse.

What I did understand, with a wrenching finality, was how badly she needed me to be the monster she had made me, how I had to be the one who dealt out 'emotional savagery' and toxicity and pain, how I was the one who distorted and changed what was said and done, how fundamentally that image of me underpinned her perceptions of herself. I also understood that, for her, my pain didn't (doesn't) exist, which was perhaps the worst thing of all.

It made clear something that I had known, underneath all our conflicts. If I were proved 'innocent' on one charge, the list of crimes would shift and dissolve and change to other accusations. I understood that there was no appeal against these accusations, that even to protest against their injustice and untruth was proof of my perfidy.

Over the next few days, I began to recognise how much I had internalised her perception of me, how it had shaped me into guilts I hadn't even realised I possessed, how in so many areas of my life it had silenced me and inhibited my actions.

I look at this monster — the monstrous me that she nurtured so carefully for so many years, since maybe from before we could speak — and I wonder how it happened. We aren't children anymore. We have children of our own, lives that we have made that extend far beyond the determinations and traumas of our childhoods. Yet here I am, back in the world of the damaged child who strikes out at hurt, unable and unwilling to perceive the lived realities of any other person.

Maybe she needs that monster. But now I know that monster is killing me.

What is this dark beast? How was she conceived?

The naming of the intolerable, John Berger once said, is itself the hope. So where I do begin?

How about me, idly tapping into Google the name of an ancestor. General Sir Beauchamp Duff, a third cousin of my grandmother, who was disgraced 'after failing to take Baghdad in 1915'. As the Scottish *Daily Record* reported in 2006, when his medals were sold at auction by Sotheby's, he was appointed Commander-in-Chief of India in 1913, the first to be appointed from the so-called Indian Army rather than the British Army. He was responsible for the war in Mesopotamia (which we now call Iraq). He sent an expeditionary force to occupy Basra in November 1914, to protect the oil interests of the Anglo-Persian Oil Company (which later turned into British Petroleum), resulting in a five-month siege at Kut al-Amara by the Ottoman Army. Thirteen thousand British troops were captured, and many of them died in Turkish prisons.

Ultimately, it was regarded as Britain's greatest military disaster, with a loss of twenty-three thousand lives.

The Mesopotamia Commission of Enquiry into the disaster was merciless. Lord Curzon condemned it as 'official blundering and incompetence' on a scale not seen since the Crimean War.

The family secret was that he killed himself, announcing his intention in a farewell letter to my grandmother. But it was widely known, even at the time: Commander Josiah Wedgwood said that the Commission of Enquiry pushed him to take his life. The *Daily Record* baldly calls him the 'suicide general'.

All these secrets that everybody knows.

The family lore says that he couldn't carry the deaths of 'his men' on his conscience, and perhaps that was part of it. But Great Uncle Bee was already responsible for so many deaths. What broke him was being the publicly mocked face of an action that Lord Kitchener called a 'calamity' for British India.

I google some more.

By 1900, in his late forties, Great Uncle Bee was the Assistant Adjutant-General on Lord Roberts' staff in South Africa, during the Second Boer War.

Under Lord Kitchener, Lord Roberts was in charge of the occupation of Pretoria. When a massive British invasion failed to defeat the Boers, who resorted to guerrilla warfare, Lord Roberts oversaw the scorched-earth policy that defeated them. The British forces burned the Boer farms and rounded up the homeless civilian population in concentration camps that lacked food, sanitation, and medical care. It wasn't the first time this tactic was used: the Spanish similarly imprisoned civilians in Cuba in 1896.

The British camps in South Africa were, however, far larger. They incarcerated more than 150,000 Africans and Boers, mostly women and children, in squalid conditions, where many of them died of disease. After the war, a report concluded that 27,927 Boers, half of whom were children under sixteen, had died in the camps. Rumours of the camps began to circulate in England, and in 1900 the South African Women and Children Distress Fund sent a three-woman delegation led by Emily Hobhouse — whom Kitchener later referred to as 'that bloody woman' — to investigate the so-called 'refuge camps'. Hobhouse called them 'a wholesale cruelty'.

In a time-honoured reflex, the British military denied any problems, and then claimed that if there were problems, it was the fault of women. The military governor of Pretoria, General John Maxwell, said that 'the inmates are well cared for, and though the death rate amongst the children is excessive, it is in most cases the fault of the mothers themselves'. A camp doctor memorably described Hobhouse and her companions as 'a few hysterical unsexed women who are prepared to sacrifice everything for notoriety'.

There was little attempt by the British or the Boers to keep records of the estimated 107,000 Africans who were interned, so precise numbers of their deaths are not available. But, says an anonymous historian on Wikipedia, 'it is thought that about 12 per cent of Black African inmates died (about 14,154)'. That seems to be a curiously conservative figure, given Africans made up two-thirds of the prisoners. I check the figures again. A historian who examined graveyards estimates the deaths at 20,000 people, 80 per cent of them children.

Although the scorched-earth policy was considered a military failure that radicalised the Boers and extended the war, Lord Roberts was showered with honours for his good work when he returned home to Britain. He was made a Knight of the Order of the Garter, Earl Roberts of Kandahar in Afghanistan and Pretoria in the Transvaal Colony and of the City of Waterford, and Viscount St Pierre. General Sir Beauchamp Duff, who was twice mentioned in dispatches, partook in the glory: he was awarded the CB and received the Queen's Medal with five clasps. This marked the beginning of his rise to prominence: after this, he became Lord Kitchener's 'trusted Adjutant-General', and eventually his successor as Commander-in-Chief of India.

The concentration camp is the symbol of twentieth-century horror. I have known for a long time that they weren't a Nazi invention, that the Nazis copied earlier models developed by the English and Americans (shortly after the former instituted concentration camps in South Africa, the latter herded tens of thousands of people into camps in the Philippines). But this feels personal. I don't know what to do with this knowledge. It curls inside me, a reflex of disgust, a chill of revulsion.

Somewhere inside me, I always knew it. There was always a little voice, whispering, *the worst has already happened*. Only the worst didn't happen to me. The worst happened to all those people. All those countless, uncounted people.

There's a logic at work here, a logic of brutalisation. Like fog, it's at once overwhelmingly obvious and difficult to grasp.

It's often argued that being brutalised inevitably leads to the brutalisation of others. This isn't true: most children who are sexually abused don't grow up to abuse others. On the other hand, most convicted paedophiles report that they suffered abuse as a child, although the researchers have a cautionary caveat: this research was conducted in prisons, and the subjects may be reporting the abuse as a mitigating factor.

There are many possible responses to brutalisation. Some people end up being extraordinarily empathic to the suffering of others. Others don't survive. Still others become abusers themselves. The outcomes are infinite. But I find myself more and more interested in one form of abuse: an ideology that conditions children from birth to consider some human beings as lesser than others.

I am, still, a British subject, uneasily resident in Australia. Until 1987, all Australians were automatically British subjects under Australian law, although not under British law — which says everything about the colonies. My forebears, all of them, were loyal servants of the British Empire, one of the biggest machineries of violence that has ever existed. And even that was only one limb of the many-tentacled phenomenon that is European colonialism and its inheritor, US imperialism. For the past few hundred years, this machinery has influenced the life of every creature on the planet. It changed the nature of human consciousness. It enslaved, impoverished, murdered, and disinherited millions of people. It demolished the natural world until it transformed the very texture of the atmosphere itself, until our very existence on the planet is endangered.

Western imperialism is indeed a staggering achievement. It's so huge, so multifaceted, that it's impossible to see whole: each of us who is part of it can see only a little, and even that through a glass darkly, because of how it polices and determines the very shapes of our thought. And I can't pretend, here or anywhere, to do anything except trace a small, wonky, uncertain line.

It's not as simple as claiming that my sister and I are estranged because of western imperialism. Nothing is that simple. We are, both of us, each of us, individuals making our choices, this way and that way, within the larger structures that determine our individual and collective histories. But I am nevertheless certain that the brutalisations that are expressed between us — the impassable void of incomprehension, the damage we did and do to each other — emerge out of the privileged subjecthood of empire.

I hesitate to claim *trauma*: trauma seems more properly claimed by the people my family colonised. Victimhood is too readily claimed by those who won't consider the people they have themselves victimised. Nevertheless, colonisation is, *necessarily*, a process of traumatisation for everyone who is born into the system. Trauma is colonisation's fuel and its machinery, its major production, its major means of production.

One of the major effects of trauma is its impact on memory. It distorts memory, falsifies, fractures, and erases it, until you can't find your way back to its origin, until everything you are is a series of responses to something that you can't remember. Sometimes this seems to me to be the entire history of what we call western civilisation.

We say, *to make sense*, which means to create a coherent pattern that is comprehensible. We say (I say): I want to see clearly. I say: I wish to illuminate, I desire to create clarity. By default, I refer to *sense* in terms of sight, which feels to me the most impersonal and distancing of the senses. Our culture thinks of the intimate senses — smell, taste, touch — as lesser authorities. *Feminine*.

What can it mean, then, to *make sense?*

Perhaps the truest way for me to make sense is to make a non-sense.

Ancestors

I join ancestry.com and begin to trace my forebears. It turns into an obsession. I can't find any trace of an Italian great-great-grandmother, an aristocrat who, according to family myth, was responsible for the 'touch of the tar brush' that made my grandmother never go out in the sun, not ever. Even when she was eighty, her skin was flawlessly white. Nor can I find any trace of the Burmese woman — a princess, of course — who supposedly married into my grandfather's family.

Perhaps nothing demonstrates heterosexist patriarchy quite as clearly as genealogical searches: the absorption of women's names into the male 'line', which must always be a line, straight and legible. It's hard to find out much about women: even the aristocratic women mainly exist as mothers, wives, daughters, siblings, names in census records, notations of birth and death and marriage. It's much easier to find out about men.

The endless gaps and questions.

For instance: my maternal grandfather's aunt Mabel Blewett, who died at twenty-three in Tokyo, having been married for a year to Alfred Arnold, who was then a seventy-one-year-old journalist. He died at 112 and was interviewed for *Time* magazine about his improbably colourful life.

In 1899, he told *Time*, Alfred was a journalist in Tokyo when hostilities broke out between the Philippines and the United States. According to the records, he married Mabel in Tokyo at this time. He said he was arrested as a spy by Filipino authorities and abandoned in the jungle to be eaten by flies, but was luckily rescued by US troops. He doesn't mention Mabel.

There is a photograph of Mabel in her bridal costume, taken in a Japanese studio. Why did she die so early? Was she too arrested as a spy? Why does Alfred not mention her? Was it, perhaps, too painful? Had he forgotten her? Or did he mention her, and the reporter decide to leave her out, because she wasn't important?

I discover Reverend Ezekiel Blomfield (1778–1818), my fourth-great-grandfather. (I find a useful table: I have sixty-four fourth-great-grandparents, and Ezekiel is responsible for 1.5 per cent of my DNA.) I feel an affinity for Ezekiel: he was, like me, mostly an autodidact, and died in poverty and ill health after a lifetime of writing. Alexander Balloch Grosart's entry on him in the Dictionary of National Biography isn't promising. '*Philosophy of History* was published in a fine quarto in 1819, with a memoir,' he says. 'It is somewhat fragmentary and commonplace. In 1807 had appeared, in two huge quartos, Blomfield's *A General View of the World, Geographical, Historical, and Philosophical; on a plan entirely new* (Bungay, 1807); this work shows wide but ill-digested reading.'

A pang of fellow feeling that is also a pang for me: here I am, with my distressingly fragmentary text, which I hope isn't too full of 'wide but ill-digested reading' or, indeed, too commonplace ... When I find Ezekiel, I wonder if he is the person I was in a waking vision I had when I was twenty-seven years old, when I was pregnant with my second child, and my relationship with the father of my children was breaking down. It was a fragment of visual memory (or fantasy, but what is the difference?) that most certainly wasn't mine. In this vision, which was very brief but deeply shaking because of its vividness and clarity, I knew several things with certainty. I was a man, and I was some kind of priest, and it was a long time ago. I was standing on a cliff looking out to sea somewhere in England, but nowhere that I, Alison, recognised, and I was twenty-seven. And I was full of a wrenching, soul-destroying regret, although I don't know what for.

It's nonsense to think that a memory of such specificity could sleep in my genes and wake in my own moment of wrenching trouble six generations later. But this vision has always puzzled me, precisely because it was so random and so specific. Perhaps I can assign this to Ezekiel, my poor, misled, troubled forebear, a man whose intellectual ambitions desired to embrace all history and thought, who had 'a talent for versification' but forswore poetry for the Revealed Truth of God and who ended up with a collection of fragments, a compiler and repository of the authorities of other men.

A drawing of Ezekiel 'by an unknown artist' is in the National Portrait Gallery in London. It dates from the early nineteenth century, when he would have been in his twenties. It shows a clean-shaven man seated in a chair, dressed in a frock coat and cravat, his short hair brushed fashionably forward. He somehow gives the impression that he is short, and his face is round and kindly, his mouth mild, his eyes large. He looks a little like my uncle Robin, my mother's brother.

All his books are on religious or philosophical themes. There's *The Life of Jesus Christ; with a history of the first propagation of the Christian religion, and the lives of the most eminent persons mentioned in the New Testament.* His *A General View of the World, Geographical, Historical, and Philosophical; on a plan entirely new; in two volumes* went into twelve editions. I find his final book, *Lectures on the Philosophy of History, accompanied with notes, and illustrative engravings*, in a facsimile edition on Amazon Kindle. Naturally, I'm consumed by curiosity and buy it. Published posthumously to raise money for Ezekiel's widowed wife and children, it turns out to be an eccentric text that seems to bear out Alexander Balloch Grosart's disdainful judgement.

The introduction outlines his life. 'His parents, though destitute of wealth, and occupying a very lowly station in society, possessed these moral and religious qualities, which infinitely exceed in value all worldly abundance. It was their first care to train up their children in the fear of God ...' The memoir describes a child who 'from infancy' had exhibited an 'insatiable desire of knowledge', who began a system of natural history and a chronology of events in the Bible before he was ten years old. It also shows a life in which 'a talent for versification' led him to something of an education from 'several benevolent individuals', but also, by raising doubts, dragged him away from the 'vital and essential truths' of Christianity.

Having wrestled down doubt, he diligently investigated Revelation, John of Patmos' apocalyptic text, and decided for God. He was given a congregation in Norfolk, and in 1800 married Mary Funnell, with whom he had a number of children. His life after that is a tale of increasing ill health, as he struggled to make an income. It included a disastrous publishing venture that left him in debt for the rest of his short life. Just as he began to see a way out of debt with a planned lecture series, he became seriously ill, perhaps with pneumonia, and his 'sudden dissolution ... took place as he was in the act of dressing himself, on the morning of the 14th July, 1818'.

The 'advertisement' in the front of *Philosophy of History* solicits the sympathy of the reader, stating 'that the following lectures, having been delivered from brief notes, were not committed to writing till the constitution of their author was so broken down by sickness, as to render him unequal to the task of transcribing, or even of revising them; that they were dictated amidst great mental languor and bodily infirmity ...' They're prefaced with a series of maps of the world. 'Nos. 1, 2,' says the 'Explanation of the Maps', 'Are coloured according to the colours of the inhabitants.' Australia, which is more or less the shape we know now, except that Tasmania is part of the mainland, is completely black. Central and northern Africa are white, like Europe; southern China is bafflingly grey; and even more bafflingly, an area inside the Arctic Circle is green.

His opening explanations are a magisterial survey of the races of the world, which are a reminder that he never in his life travelled any great distance from his native Norfolk. He cites Moses, the author of the Pentateuch, as his major authority 'as to the early history of mankind', so I guess we know where we are. The racism is totally yikes, but is of a piece with the taxonomies current at the time, notably Linnaeus', with some interesting differences: as a Congregational minister, he was an abolitionist, and reserves hard words for the scum Europeans enslaving Africans, whom he places in their civilised status next to Europeans. He seems to reserve his highest moral disapproval for Laplanders and other races inside the Arctic Circle, who are 'altogether unfit for military service', and 'barbarians' such as the Native Americans, of whom he recites the standard libels. The capacity for military achievement is central to his theories about the hierarchies of the races: war, he argues, is a central civilising influence. At least, the proper kind of war.

Ezekiel's book as a whole seems especially anxious to distinguish the wars of civilised races, which promulgate civilisation, from those of barbarians. 'Civilized nations, which take arms upon cool reflection ... carry on their hostilities with so little rancour or animosity, that war among them is disarmed of half its terrors,' he notes. 'Barbarians are strangers to such refinements.'

I wonder what Ezekiel's conception of this lack of rancour or animosity actually is. I think of Goya's etchings *The Disasters of War*, which catalogued some of the atrocities of the Peninsular War, when Napoleon invaded Spain, a conflict that had ended only two years before Ezekiel delivered his lectures. 'Plate 34: *Por una navaja* (*For a clasp knife*). A garrotted priest grasps a crucifix in his hands.' 'Plate 9: *No quieren* (*They do not want to*). An elderly woman wields a knife in defence of a young woman who is being assaulted by a soldier.' *The Third of May 1808*, the famous image in which Spanish resisters are executed by Napoleon's military.

I study this mild-faced cleric's portrait again. A kindly man, by all accounts. Somehow, I don't doubt it. Empires have often been built on the speculations of kindly, Godly men.

Ezekiel would have been keenly interested in the Napoleonic Wars, which devastated Europe for more than a decade during his adult life. They were the first of the 'total wars', which transformed the entirety of the nations that participated in them. They sparked the beginnings of European nationalism, the rise of Britain as the world's most powerful empire, and not uncoincidentally, the escalation in status of Ezekiel's descendants, loyal servants of Britain.

At the back of the book is a list of those who subscribed to the publication. It's a long list, featuring a lot of clerics, a few women ('Ludlow, Miss, Sudbury'), and a Brett, John, Esq. of East India House, the headquarters of the East India Company.

So many of my forebears were not born in England. I'm almost shocked by how the facts of their births lay bare the extent of the British Empire. My paternal grandmother was born in Calcutta, India, in 1910. Her father, Lieutenant Albert George Thompson, a surgeon who served in the medical corps in the Boer War and India, was born and died in England. My maternal great-grandmother, Annie Grace, was born in Singapore or Java, as were her siblings, one of which was Mabel. My maternal grandfather was born in Sandakan, Borneo, in 1899. His siblings were born in Singapore, the Malay States, Devon, Perranporth, Bishop's Stortford. The Stevens family, my maternal grandmother's father's family, were almost all born in Bengal: Balghupar, Arrah, Kishnaghur. My uncle Stanley was born in Khartoum, Sudan. My uncle Robin was born in Gibraltar. I and my sisters were born in South Africa in the 1960s.

And so on. The diaspora of the conquerors, who must head out to the colonies to bring them into order, to gather the wealth and bring it home.

Almost all my nineteenth-century ancestors were middle- or upper-class foot soldiers of empire. In some cases, they were captains, generals, admirals, governors. Others were engineers, doctors, miners, administrators. I'm speaking of the men, because I can't find out much about the women.

At one point, I almost get excited, when I discover that my grandfather's father was born in a workhouse and died in a lunatic asylum. Perhaps here is something not quite so irredeemably privileged? But alas, his father was actually the master of the Fulham Workhouse, so when the census records his presence there, it's not as an inmate. He died in a lunatic asylum, and my mother tells me that he reportedly had syphilis, which fits with the extant facts. It's a tragic and horrible death, but speaks little to redemption.

I thumb through a box of photographs. There's a small black-and-white photo of my Uncle Tiny as a boy. He's photographed at a play campsite set up in an English garden, and he's lying belly down at the entrance of a two-man tent. Next to him is a dog with cropped ears, and he's holding a rifle that he's pointing at a tiger. The tiger has been made into a rug, its mouth frozen open in a roar. On the back is written, I don't know by whom, perhaps my uncle Robin: 'Tiny (note left handed)'. So there is left-handedness on two sides of my family. I didn't know until my youngest son turned out to be left-handed that it existed in our family at all. I didn't know that my father was forced to write with his right hand at school.

Another photo of the same scene, this time with Robin, also pointing a gun at the dead tiger. This one is printed as a postcard, and written on the back is 'Robin and Tiny. Tiger shooting. Ashton 1935 (?)' So it was taken in England, perhaps in the village of Ashton in Cambridgeshire, just before the war. Tiny was then eleven and he only had six more years to live: he died at seventeen, newly appointed to HMS Hood when it went down into the cold Atlantic in one of the major naval losses of World War II.

I wonder why people made rugs out of tigers. I stare at it:

it's so grotesque. A dead animal to walk on while drinking tea.

There is a series of photographs from India from around 1900. On the backs are written 'Uncle Harry and Aunt Helena'. Harry is Henry Herbert Stevens, my great-uncle, the son of Charles Cecil Stevens, Knight Commander of the Most Exalted Order of the Star of India, and briefly, from 1897 to 1898, Lieutenant Governor of Bengal.

These photos are almost parodies: they portray a group of English people, mostly men but including Aunt Helena, all of them wearing pith helmets. In one image, they're posed under a tree, staring expressionlessly into the camera, the image of British colonists. Behind them stand Indians, some in western dress, two Sikhs in traditional dress. 'Unknown companions', says a note on the back of another photo of Harry and Helena, referring to the Indians. In another photograph, the English are sitting around a picnic blanket. A white-robed, dark-skinned man is bending over, offering one of them something to eat out of what looks like a saucepan. In the background is a dog that looks like a pointer; behind the dog stretch undulating hills covered with trees. These photos were, according to the unknown notator, taken at Shikan camp. I google, but the only place called Shikan that I can find is in China. Tibet?

How many people died because of my family? How many crimes were their hands part of? How much did they steal? How many languages did they erase, how many cultures did they trample, how many people did they enslave, beat, torment, murder? How do you quantify this?

Great Uncle Bee, the Suicide General, the Disaster of Mesopotamia. General Sir Beauchamp Duff, Knight Grand Cross of the Most Honourable Order of the Bath, Knight Grand Commander of the Most Exalted Order of the Star of India, Knight Commander of the Royal Victorian Order, Companion of the Most Eminent Order of the Indian Empire, Knight of Justice of the Order of St John, was, without doubt, personally responsible for more than a few deaths. Impersonally, he was responsible for thousands more.

I try to do a reckoning of this one ancestor, among the more prominent of all my colonial forebears who worked in the bureaucracy that looted India, transforming it from one of the wealthiest countries in the world to one of the poorest, transferring all that wealth to the treasuries and country mansions of England.

(We looted the language too: 'loot', according to the Collins English Dictionary, was stolen from Hindi in the nineteenth century: lūṭ. The Online Etymology Dictionary explains that it means 'goods taken from an enemy, etc.', 1788, Anglo-Indian, from Hindi lut, from Sanskrit loptram, lotram 'booty, stolen property', from PIE *roup-tro-, from root *reup- 'to snatch'. The verb is first attested 1821, from the noun.)

Even as I begin, I don't know how to narrow down my accounting. As with the vague reports of the Africans in the concentration camps in the Boer War, the British often didn't bother to list the deaths of Black or brown people.

According to Wikipedia, one of Great Uncle Bee's early actions was as Deputy Assistant Adjutant-General during the Waziristan campaign between 1894 and 1895. Waziristan, now part of Pakistan, is an arid mountainous region, hot in summer and snowbound in winter, that lies along the Afghanistan border. The conflict was sparked by the British creating a border, the Durand Line, that was to divide Afghanistan and the tribal areas. The Pathan population of Waziristan objected to the border, as they correctly assumed this was the first stage of a British takeover of their homes.

In November 1894, two thousand Mahsud tribesmen, led by a radical Muslim preacher called Mullah Powindah, attacked eight thousand British troops before dawn at Wano, taking the British by surprise.

The success of this attack put a huge dent in British prestige, so clearly retribution had to follow. Great Uncle Bee (GUB) fought in the action at Wano and was twice mentioned in dispatches. This signalled his promotion to Brevet Lieutenant-Colonel. He was also part of the punitive expeditions that followed through Mahsud country, under General Lockhart, to whom GUB was later Military Secretary.

I squint at the facsimiles of military reports I find in digital libraries online and begin to feel lost. I read accounts of the punitive expeditions. 'General Lockhart accompanied the Second Brigade to the Mahsud town of Makin, on the way destroying the village of the Mullah Powindah, Marobi. There was random shooting, but no significant resistance ...' They outline British surveys into what is now Pakistan and Afghanistan: the locals resisted, resulting in reprisals in which villages were burned and 'cattle seized'.

Finally, most of the Pathan tribes capitulated to the British. Mullah Powindah evaded capture and continued to preach jihad against the British in Waziristan through the 1890s, reportedly leading other guerrilla attacks, before he died in 1913.

So that was the beginning of that particular mess. And the beginning of GUB's career — which led him to the Second Boer War in South Africa, where he helped to prosecute the policy of concentration camps against the Boers and Africans, so that he came to the attention of Lord Kitchener, after which he rose through the ranks and became Commander-in-Chief of India.

That this was the first time the Indian Army was led by a man risen from its own ranks seems to represent a shift in power. No doubt seeking to capitalise on the new authority of the colonial army, GUB was one of the major decision-makers behind the 1914 expeditionary force to Basra. The wide-ranging government inquiry into the Mesopotamian catastrophe would later say, 'it looked as if India were trying to lay down a policy behind the back of the Secretary of State and the Cabinet'. Although the surrender to the Ottoman Army was one of the biggest humiliations of British history, perhaps GUB's greater crime was his attempt to wrest control from Whitehall. Perhaps if he had been a general for the British Army, it might have gone down as a glorious defeat, rather than a crime.

The British effectively took control after the war ended, importing civil servants from India to administer the region and negotiating the British Mandate for Mesopotamia in 1920. According to at least one contemporary commentator, H.C. Armstrong, 'England wanted Mosul and its oil. The Kurds were the key'.

The casualties of the entire Mesopotamia campaign are staggering. Altogether 85,197 British soldiers died, and an estimated 325,000 Ottoman soldiers. Most of the deaths on both sides were from disease. The wider casualties of war — the destruction of civilian lives, landscapes, towns, histories, records, cultures — are mostly unrecorded. The histories are being rewritten, old atrocities dug up, old crimes reconsidered. But the full toll will never be accurately calculated.

It all seems so desolately familiar. In the twenty-first century, we're fighting the same wars that were fought last century: I read the names of the same towns, the same regions. Is it worse now? How can you measure 'worse'?

Murder, Jean Genet said, is an absolute crime: and you can't multiply absolutes.

Even with my amateurish genealogical skills, I'm able to trace forebears back to the twelfth century. The fact that they're traceable means that they're self-selecting: the titled ancestors exist in records, while the less noble branches of the thickening, bewildering tree trickle off into obscurity. In the end, I just push the way of least resistance, tracing a patrilineal line back to one Laird Freskin 'The Fleming' Sutherland, First Lord of Duffus, who is my twenty-first-great-grandfather. Mathematics tells me that he is one of 8,388,608 possible grandparents of that generation, although mathematics is clearly mitigated by cousinly marriages. This side of the family tracks back to Scotland through Duffs, Dunbars, Frasers, Sutherlands, a plethora of baronetcies, earldoms, lairds, ladies …

Laird Freskin, also known as Hugh de Moravia, was born around 1107. I can't find anything more on ancestry.com, so I begin to google, and fall down a rabbit hole of medieval European politics and family legends (always the family legends). What seems to emerge solidly from the fog is that Freskin, along with many other Flemish colonisers, was a strategic part of David I's suppression of the Gaelic lords of Scotland.

Freskin's rise to wealth and power came after the defeat of Óengus of Moray, the last mormaer (king) of Moray, a large polity in what is now north-east Scotland. Óengus' claim to the Scottish throne was traced through his maternal grandfather, Lulach mac Gille Coemgáin: his full Gaelic title was Oenghus mac inghine Lulaich, ri Moréb (Angus the son of the daughter of Lulach, ruler of Moray). I can't find any record of Óengus' mother's name; she is merely the vessel of succession. Lulach's mother, on the other hand, is famous: she was a queen of Scotland called Gruoch ingen Boite. She was married twice. Her first husband, Lulach's father, was the mormaer of Moray Gille Coemgáin. Her second was a Scottish king called MacBethad mac Findlaích, better known to us as Macbeth. After Macbeth was killed in the Battle of Lumphanan in 1057, Lulach was crowned king at Scone. He lasted only a few months before he was assassinated by Malcolm III, who then usurped the throne. David I was Malcolm III's son.

In 1130, according to the English chronicler Orderic Vitalis, Óengus and Máel Coluim mac Alaxandair, another pretender to the throne, marched into Gaelic Scotia from Moray with five thousand warriors (Vitalis makes clear he considers it an 'invasion', although elsewhere it's characterised as a rebellion). They were utterly defeated by David I's forces under the generalship of Edward Siwardsson at the Battle of Stracathro. Óengus was killed in the fight, which according to the Anglo-Saxon Chronicle was 'a great slaughter', with some sources saying that four thousand men died. After that battle, David I's forces took over Moray and distributed it among various loyal nobles, including Freskin, who was given Strathbrock in West Lothian, as well as Duffus, Roseisle, Inchikel, Machir, and Kintrae in Moray. This secured these lands under the authority of the Crown.

Charles Rampini's 1898 *A History of Moray and Nairn* gives an excellent colonial version of suppressing the 'tribes', using language recognisable from a thousand colonial texts:

> the Men of Moray, a warlike and impetuous race, were a thorn in the side of the Scottish kings. By alliance with others of their kind they had become a powerful body — a great tribe, in fact, consisting of many different clans, yet all in some way or another connected with the Lorn Kings of Dalriada, from whom their first maormors had sprung. Attempts to introduce law and order amongst them had hitherto been in vain. With Celtic tenacity they clung to their old wild ways, and cherished their old warlike habits

as if these constituted a moral code of infallible excellence. They were seriously retarding the progress of national civilisation, and not only so, but rapidly becoming a danger to the State.

As so often, there are dubious genealogies that link Freskin with royalty: I find several that list Freskin's father as the Comte Ollec de Flandre, II (Robert II, Count of Flanders, also known, ominously, as Robert of Jerusalem and Robert the Crusader, because he participated in Pope Urban II's First Crusade).

Resisting the lure of the bewildering histories and conflicts of petty European kings of the Holy Roman Empire, I find a 1996 paper by historian Lauran Toorians, 'Flemish Settlements in Twelfth-Century Scotland'. 'Flemings in twelfth-century Scotland,' says Toorians. 'No-one doubts their existence, and yet no-one has ever been able to tell their story.' He sketches an economic and political background of the presence of Flemings — who may have been from many parts of Europe, or who may have simply been Flemish speakers — in Scotland and Wales. He cautions that the records are scarce.

Stripped of mythic adornments, it seems a banal story, in this case driven by the highly lucrative Flemish cloth trade. 'That wool from Scotland, and even more important, from England, was essential for the cloth industry in Flanders from about 1100 is common historical knowledge,' says Toorians. He notes that Flemings acted as colonists all over Europe, including in the British Isles. He also notes that they were much in demand as mercenaries and were bold and cruel in battle. 'That in Scotland this employment was known as well, is confirmed by [Anglo-Norman poet and historian] Jordan Fantosme, who described how King William asked to

> ... send us from Flanders his Flemings with ships
> By hundreds and by fifties of those bold people:
> I will give them the road to the people who war against us,
> They will attack the castles by regular siege.'

This seems the most likely provenance for Freskin, 'an adventurous Fleming' of uncertain ancestry. Toorians writes that the 'plantation of Moray' with Norman settlers occurred in 1163. Flemings were welcomed as new settlers without traditional ties to the region, to break the old alliances of the native population or earlier rulers and so bring the area more securely within the power of the Scottish kings. 'The words which have suggested wholesale transference of population in 1163 are vague: *rex Malcolmus Muraviensis transtulit* ... But Fordun refers to the action taken as drastic, though justified by the continued unrest.' I go down another rabbit hole via Marjorie Ogilvie Anderson's commentary on the Chronicle of Holyrood. She tells me Fordun's history is 'very imaginative'.

> The Chronicle of Holyrood may perhaps be understood to mean that there was an extension in Moray of the policy of plantation, which had possibly begun there before ... and that this extension resulted from a rebellion in Moray, possibly after king Malcolm's homage at Woodstock. But the words may also mean other things. It would even be difficult to say with certainty that they cannot mean

'translated men of Moray' who had suffered martyrdom, or 'changed the place of [the bishops] of Moray' ... To build upon any interpretation of the words would be exceedingly unsafe.

So here I am again, sinking into another mire of uncertainty and contradiction. However, it seems most historians agree that after the defeat of Óengus, there was a 'plantation' of Norman settlers in Scotland. 'Both in Wales and in Scotland, they seem to have come not so much as cultivators, but more as sheep-breeders and wool-merchants,' says Toorians.

Freskin was a major beneficiary of this colonisation and — reflecting no doubt a continuing resistance to the colonists — his family was responsible for the building of the greatest motte, or earth fortress, in the province at Duffus. All we really know about Freskin, says Toorians,

is that his son William was confirmed by William the Lion in the lands which were given to Freskin by David I. His family became very powerful in Moray, and his sons adopted the name de Moravia, Murray. His son Hugh was given, or perhaps only confirmed in, the territory of Sutherland by the king, and his grandson, known as Willelmus de Moravia, *miles* and *dominus de Suthyrlandia*, became the first Earl of Sutherland in about 1230.

At this point, I understand that, although I hadn't consciously realised it, I have been searching for some kind of pre-colonialist history on which I can hang the beginning of a hat, as if there were some kind of Edenic innocence that might absolve the later histories. As soon as I realise this, I feel deeply foolish. Even if there were, it wouldn't make any difference to me, now, in the twenty-first century, trawling through libraries half a world away through histories I only superficially understand.

No doubt among those millions of remote ancestors are some of those rebellious Gaels, the anonymous poor and dispossessed who lost the gamble of history. But they have been shaved off the narrative, like the daughters of kings who only exist to 'continue the line'. It's the cultural memory that counts here, the myths that are continually reinforced over centuries, wearing a path through the same old story of conquest, erasure, and entitlement; these patterns that shape a million family histories in a tiny, cold, bellicose northern-hemisphere island.

I wonder about the structures of thought and feeling that have been shaped by this linear history, which names itself the 'progress of civilisation'. I wonder about the stories that never made it into official histories — because they were ignored or destroyed, or because they were never written down, as those who knew the stories didn't know how to write. When they died, their stories were forgotten with them. Those voiceless ghosts, only audible in their absences.

The fracture

I have often thought writing to be a cold act, a hammer on hot iron. In order to write at all, I must split my self into she who feels and she who writes.

There's a reason why writing seems to me to be a kind of blasphemy. It translates the world into abstract patterns that then become their own reality. The fluid breath becomes unmoving marks on a page, amorphous internal thoughts are hammered into an object. In this way, it's similar to how money abstracts the real, appropriating all authentic being to itself. The *real* was the name of a small Spanish silver coin, which itself derives from regal, or royal. We still say *real estate*, indicating the real as property, as tradable object.

Perhaps this is what Wallace Stevens meant when he said that poetry is a kind of money.

But I persist, nevertheless, in believing that writing can also be an attempt at freedom, a struggle to recognise and break confining patterns. The desire to write is for me wound into the desire to open a different way of being that exists in my body, somewhere deep in my physical memory. I glimpse that other way in still moments, watching the sky maybe or in the middle of a task. And once in childbirth, when my conscious mind was flailing in panic, and another kind of knowing stepped forward: an exact, small, clear voice that knew precisely what was happening.

Absent voices crowd in my throat, a world of quivering, diverse, repressed life. It feels like a function of trauma, like the vivid plague dreams that weave through the narratives of the pandemic. All those lost selves, all those forgotten memories, all those stories that were stamped out, that were labelled 'old wives' tales', 'fairytales', that were dismissed as lies.

The story of the fracture, which is the central story of the colonialist self.

I think of Arthur Rimbaud, the precocious bisexual teenage poet who became an icon of modernity, maybe the most startling example of a truncated self. In literary histories, he shapes his legendary, meteoric adolescence with a fierce, pitiless intelligence: he speaks of the derangement of the senses, the lures of addiction, the blazing banners of revolution. And then when he was twenty, he decided to write no more poems. Instead, he became an exemplary colonist. In 1876, he joined the Dutch Colonial Army for the sum of three hundred florins and was sent to Java; he soon deserted and a few years later tried to cross the Alps. He finally ended up in Africa, where, his biographer Graham Robb says, he was prone to 'sudden eruptions of rage and peculiar violence'. He ended up as a coffee merchant and arms dealer in present-day Somalia and Ethiopia, sending back several reports to the French Société de Géographie, which at one point wrote asking to include him in their list of famous geographers and explorers (Rimbaud never answered). As Edward Said noted, all territories must be mapped to be possessed.

According to Robb, Rimbaud was a very successful businessman. The legend of his financial failures, so neatly moralising in the legend of the poète maudit, is apparently a sham: as with many a corporation before and after him, he fiddled the numbers. He was, his business acquaintances said, a 'good accountant': he made large profits and turned even his own misfortunes into opportunities. He died of bone cancer in his leg in 1891, when he was thirty-seven. He rejected fame, as he rejected so many other things, but fame came to him, all the same, clustering thickly around the absences he began to represent.

Rimbaud visited unspeakable violence on the bodies of others, and on his own body. As an adolescent, his flesh was the site of atrocious neglect. When as a child poet he stayed with the poet Paul Verlaine, Verlaine's wife complained about the louse-ridden sheets. His poems, which spoke to me so vividly a century later, burn with violence. In 'The Poet Aged Seven', he writes about the gaze of his mother (his unyielding mother, who bullied him into his genius — sweating 'with obedient zeal' while his orientalising imagination dreamed of deserts of freedom, apocalyptic banners of revolution, the brown-eyed daughter of 'the working folk next door'). She had, he wrote, 'le bleu regard, — qui ment!' — the blue-eyed stare — which lies! Poor Madame Rimbaud, Widow Rimbaud, as she called herself, abandoned to raise her children alone. She has been judged much more harshly than her son.

Rimbaud was also speaking of his own eyes. His best friend Ernest Delahaye said they were 'pale blue irradiated with dark blue — the loveliest eyes I've seen'. *The blue-eyed stare that lies.*

The narrative of Rimbaud's colonial life is dank with crime: manslaughter, fraud, possible murder. Most horribly, there's a brief account of the rape of an infibulated child who 'entered his house'. 'Rimbaud set about things a little too bluntly and when he came across the aforementioned obstacle, he attempted to cut it out with a knife.' Bizarrely, Robb describes this incident as a 'shaft of daylight', in reference to Rimbaud's sexuality. It's 'uncorroborated', as most rapes are, although the men who repeated the anecdote otherwise spoke well of Rimbaud. The incident, they said, 'almost ended badly'.

It ended badly for the girl, without question. What happened to her? A dismissive line in a later letter suggests that she may have been called Méram. In the story of Rimbaud, she exists as part of a colourful, exotic colonial background, a frisson of monstrousness that gives an edge to a man often sentimentally portrayed as a Romantic antihero. The contemporary account of the incident has an edge of humour, as if this were merely an unfortunate incident. The girl? Who cares about the girl? No one. Or at least, no one who matters.

Robb comments, 'Rimbaud's poetry is such a memorable application of the cherished injunction "Know thyself" that it is hard to accept the results of the experiment and to conclude that literature is the guardian of culture only if it never tries to leave the page … Excuses made for Rimbaud are also excuses for the colonial project as a whole …'

In her essay 'Brexit, the Body & the Politics of Splitting', psychologist Guilaine Kinouani writes about the split self, the Eurocentric division between body and soul that, she says, reduces our apprehension of racism 'and indeed the embodiment of all socio-historical forces'. 'This splitting goes much further though than mind and body,' she says. 'It is also present in the separation of bodies from social structures, and the extraction of the past from the present.'

> Splitting as a result does more than just sustain white ignorance. It is a vehicle for whiteness thus white violence. Once you learn to split as your primary defense when navigating the world, it becomes almost automatic not only to disconnect from your own body, your embodied experiences but also from that of others, including the pain and violence you inflict upon them. The centrality of splitting in the reproduction of racial violence cannot be overstated. Whiteness survived all historical atrocities it produced by splitting.
>
> It is splitting that allowed White people to hang Black bodies on trees and take selfies or have picnics on lynching sites. It is splitting that enabled slave masters to cherish

Black children 'as their own', then inflict the most horrific sexual violence and torture upon them for the most minor of 'infractions', seconds later. It is splitting again that meant colonialists could hold onto the bible in one hand and a rifle in the other; say a prayer then go on mass murder sprees.

Rimbaud is an exemplary colonial subjectivity. His one virtue, perhaps, was his bottomless cynicism: he never pretended that he was promoting the cause of civilisation. He saw the colonial project exactly for what it was: a rich field for an intelligent grifter with an eye for the main chance. His poems, all of them, are the traumatic splintering of that consciousness as it becomes aware of what it is. But Rimbaud never saw past that moment of violence. He merely repeated it.

Méram, if her name was Méram, doesn't count as a life — but more, she doesn't count as a consciousness. The trauma inflicted on her body, on her self, on her life, is only considered interesting as an insight into the sexuality of a famous man. Beneath all that colour: a traumatised child, a raped, mutilated girl, who becomes an uncertain footnote in the biography of the brutalised colonial self. A life that never counted at all in the annals of 'civilisation', except to Méram herself.

There is no excuse. Sorrow is beyond inadequate. No apology will do.

I cannot imagine her, because for me to do so — for me, petty scion of a colonial empire, to raise her from the dead to expiate my own trivial sadness — is only to compound the outrages committed against her. I haven't the right. But I can't forget her either.

I don't know how not to reproduce the same act, how not to make her a footnote in my own account of this fracture. Maybe the truth is that I can't do anything except repeat the same crime, over and over again. The same old curse.

Visions

This writing isn't about my sister. It's a kind of fetish, a poor substitute for reality, as all language is. I have no idea who she is, and I can no longer imagine it. This *she* is a fiction, just as the *I* she describes to me is, just as the *I* who writes these words is making a fiction of herself.

There is no end to human ingenuity.

I find myself looking for reasons, as if reasonableness were any part of this, even though I know reason is why I have always misunderstood her. My pain, her pain, our unhappiness: what do any of these have to do with reason? My desire for explanation, as if, once the reason is understood, I can relax, feeling that the problem is solved. Even if I did unwind some kind of reason, it still wouldn't really function as an explanation. All I find are other questions.

I want to resist psychology, although I read it: encyclopae-dias, books, endless webpages and forums on pop psychology. For all their crudities, they offer some kind of legibility: I recognise patterns of behaviour and feel reassured that our relationship is part of a larger structure. But if I give these behaviours a name, it feels the same as sealing them into a box, neatly labelled. Diagnosis becomes too easily a substitute for understanding.

In any case, the only thing that grants me any right to my speculations is the damage she has caused me. And that is a slender claim, easily compromised by revenge. And true, sometimes I do wish for revenge. Sometimes my anger is overwhelming: I am scorched by the sense of injustice, by frustration, the impossibility of finding any kind of solution. There is nowhere to put this anger. It rushes into a void, a cataract of confusion.

In stories as we know them, conflict always resolves one way or another: the opponents struggle either towards a luminous moment of understanding, or towards the annihi-lation of one of them (the evil one). Sometimes both of these resolutions occur at once. But this is not a story and it doesn't have a resolution, and neither understanding nor annihilation is possible.

All I know is that everything is connected. One thing led to another, which led to another, which led to another. Only it's not linear: there are so many forces at work that it's hard to trace which thing is which.

I'm a few years overdue for an eye appointment. This is bad, because I have the kind of extreme myopia that is prone to retinal detachment — which is to say, if I don't keep an eye on my eyes, I might go blind. And even though optometrists tell me that the health of my eyes is surprisingly good for a person as short-sighted as I am, I can't afford to dice with my sight.

I did anyway: because I am bad at self-care, because glasses with my prescription are so expensive. But a sudden flurry of ophthalmic migraines has finally prompted me to make an appointment. These are episodes in which flashing hexagonal threads, something like those old schematic illustrations of carbon molecules in science books for children, pulse across my vision. There's no pain, apparently because there are no nerve receptors inside the eye. The zigzagging auras make me feel nauseous, and they certainly get in the way of seeing things.

The first time this happened, maybe in my twenties, I had an extreme episode: the flashing was so dazzling I couldn't see anything else. For those ten minutes, I panicked, convinced that something terrible had happened and that I was going blind.

I first got glasses when I was eight, ugly pink-rimmed spectacles with lenses like the bottom of bottles. I hated them — once, to the ire of my parents, I even stamped on them and broke them into pieces. Those were the days when a girl with glasses was called 'Four Eyes', teased and mocked, and for me they were the visible symbol of everything I hated about myself.

In my early twenties, I mostly didn't wear them, even though I didn't yet have contact lenses. Mostly, I could fake my way through. I recognised friends by their gait, not their faces, although if they were on the other side of the street, I didn't see them at all. I couldn't read street signs, so I had to work out where I was by memorising routes.

When I first began to do public appearances like poetry readings, not wearing glasses was actually useful, because I couldn't see the audience. Being looked at by many people terrified me: I suspect that part of me believes that visibility is profoundly perilous. I still find public appearances difficult and exhausting, as if the gaze is a vampiric thing that sucks out all my energy, but being able to see people looking at me doesn't frighten me anymore.

Glasses revealed a visual world that I didn't know existed: trees that thrust out into intricate branches tipped with individual leaves, legible blackboards, the detail of grass blades. I still remember that first day, sitting in the back of a car staring out the window in wonder at the unblurred world.

So for me, right from the beginning, sight was a relative thing. Perhaps this accounts in part for my sometimes worrying negative capability, the ability to hold different contradictory thoughts at the same time. I know that things can be at once blurred and unblurred, and that the difference between the two is the careful placement of a ground pane of glass.

Perceiving the difference between the blurred and unblurred led to my realising that my vision changes all the time. I mostly tracked these shifts as emotional. Depression literally makes colours dull: objects become insubstantial, as if their very existence is vertiginous. Or those epiphanies in which everything is profoundly coloured, where the sight of autumn leaves on a wet pavement is dazzling, burning auburn on a vibrant slate grey, and the sky so deeply translucent blue I can almost believe in heaven.

In those epiphanic moments, sight feels to me like a dimension of touch. I'm aware that light is touching the objects I see, that it bounces off me and makes me seen. Everything is connected, intimately, to me. Sight extends the self to embrace the entire visible world. My eldest son, when he was two, holding out his hands to the sky: *My sky! My sea!* To see is to possess.

I can almost believe in Aquinas' notion that the eye is made of water so that the attributes of light and colour may exist within the eye itself. That vision is the ultimate sense with which we comprehend God. But I don't believe in God. And these anthropocentric optical theories — there are so many of them, all so elegant and yet so wrong — are seductive. They underpin, even as they've been rendered ridiculous by modern optics, so many of our cultural assumptions about perception.

Mostly, they reveal that vision is the least modest of the senses. Vision is greedy. Sight is the sense of the coloniser, who 'like stout Cortez ... with eagle eyes ... star'd at the Pacific'. It's what empowers the romantic traveller posed on top of a mountain in sublime thought, or the king in his tower commanding all he sees. It's the schematic map that overlays its reality of borders and roads across a landscape of scintillating micro-environments, erasing them. It's the alienated drone operator in his room, untouched by the 'baser' senses, blowing a body into oblivion.

It's the man staring at a painting of a nude woman, behind

which is represented in cunning perspective his domain, his house and lands.

Us colonists, we need to better value the gradations of blindness, to track how they reveal modes of perception that are less hierarchical, less possessive. If we are to survive the crisis that all of us have created, choice by choice by choice, we need to place ourselves in our worlds more modestly.

Vision is routinely designated as a *masculine* sense. Men, we are told, are visual animals. If you google 'men visual', every single article that comes up is about sex. The platitudes roll out as bedrock wisdom. 'When it comes to sex, men are visual animals.' 'Men are by nature visual consumers.' 'Surveys show …' 'Testosterone makes men more aware of and more aroused by what they see.' Oh really?

It's almost as if, all their lives, men are taught to look and women are taught to be looked at. But this is a gross simplification of a question that is of dizzying complexity. There are, obviously, physiological differences between people designated male and female: the ones we notice most are primary and secondary sexual characteristics and socially conditioned behaviours. The default is to push these differences into 'opposites' and assign various attributions on either side of the binary as 'natural'. Men are hard, women are soft; men are intellectual, women are emotional; men are strong, women are weak; and so on through every human quality we can name.

Untangling social and biological determination is profoundly fraught: it's a truism that the observer changes the field of perception, and never more so than in the consideration of human categorisations such as race, gender, and sex. The assumed binary of the sexes underlies almost everything that we collectively 'know' as a culture about men and women. It conditions what we 'see' because, like blinkers on a horse, it determines where we look.

Take testosterone, for instance. In popular science, it is considered the male hormone par excellence, the essence of masculinity, which sidesteps the fact that women also have testosterone in their bodies, if at lower levels. Apparently, like many things about women, its function in women is 'less well understood'.

'On the Effects of Testosterone on Brain Behavioral Functions', for example, an interesting 2015 paper by three neuroscientists — Peter Celec, Daniela Ostatníková, and Július Hodosy — evaluates a swathe of experiments on people, rodents, and monkeys. 'The results,' say the authors, 'are, unfortunately, controversial and puzzling.' The scientists examine experiments that seek to explain gendered differences — the higher incidence of anxiety in women, for example, and its different aetiology — by the presence of higher or lower levels of testosterone. The experiments they canvas often show contradictory results: while they conclude that experiments on rats and mice have demonstrated that higher levels of testosterone correlate with lower levels of anxiety, an experiment on rhesus monkeys — which should be noted, as monkeys are physiologically closer to humans — showed no such thing.

Investigations into the link between testosterone and depression are more contradictory. (Some depressed women had high levels of testosterone, for example.) 'Whether testosterone plays a major role in the sex differences in depression is unclear, but a number of studies indicate that it can affect the mood of depressive patients,' although some experiments indicate that perhaps depression lowers the level of testosterone, rather than the absence of testosterone causing depression. Even the studies on spatial abilities, designed to explain why men generally perform better, are inconclusive. 'Cultural differences, sex, and age,' they conclude, 'have all been shown to impact the physiological effects of testosterone … Most of the published literature agrees on the fact that testosterone is anxiolytic, anti-depressant, and improves spatial abilities. But this picture is oversimplified. Many variables add to the complex interactions between testosterone and the brain.'

Humans are complex, right down to the micromanaging of our hormones.

Another paper, by Heather A. Rupp and Kim Wallen, 'Sex Differences in Response to Visual Sexual Stimuli: a review', looks at the plethora of studies that attempt to define the differences between men and women in response to visual sexual stimuli. It seems that men and women are in fact both erotically aroused by visual stimuli, but they respond differently, for both biological and social reasons. Sexual response is measured through subjective ratings (subjects report their response), which the authors describe as 'an emergent product of the combined cognitive and peripheral physiological states of an individual. The cognitive contributions to sexual arousal are not completely known, but involve the appraisal and evaluation of the stimulus, categorization of the stimulus as sexual, and affective response.' The physiological response, on the other hand, is the 'physiological component of sexual arousal', including 'changes in cardiovascular function, respiration, and genital response, erection in men, and vaso-congestion in women'. As it turns out, the two responses are often different: someone may be physiologically aroused but subjectively unaroused. And self-reporting, as this intriguing snippet demonstrates, is often unreliable:

A recent study found that men characterized by high levels of hypermasculinity and ambivalent sexism reported more sexual partners when they had a female experimenter administering the anonymous survey, than if they had a male experimenter. This effect was only observed, however, when the cover page of the survey contained a statement saying that women were recently shown to be more sexually permissive and experienced than men. The findings that males who identify more strongly with traditionally masculine ideals alter their reporting when there is a message of dominant female sexuality, and that they do so only in the presence of a female experimenter, highlights the complex influence of socialized norms and attitudes on accurate reports of sexual behavior in men. These studies together emphasize the differential and polarizing effects that socialization appears to have on men and women in their reports of sexual behavior, which is important to consider when investigating sex differences in response to sexual stimuli.

Women, on the other hand, tend to under-report their subjective arousal, perhaps because of social conditioning that inhibits sexual response.

Neurological response throws up one clear difference: 'in response to erotic films, men and women showed many areas of overlap in response to sexual stimuli in the anterior cingulate, medial prefrontal cortex, orbital prefrontal cortex, insula, amygdala, thalamus, and ventral striatum. However, only men showed increased activation in the hypothalamus.' Some speculate that this is to do with the heavy lifting of the penis into erection, but the researchers say this is unlikely, because it only happens during visual stimulation, not during orgasm.

They conclude that the 'origins of the sexually differentiated response to sexual stimuli are unknown. Possible factors could be sociological, evolutionary, physiological, psychological, or most likely a combination.' In any case, the sociological effects on sexual response play a major part:

Historically, Western culture has given men more sexual freedom and constrained women more in the display of sexual motivation or interest in sexual material, a double standard that exists even to some degree today ... The social teachings experienced by men and women throughout their lives may mediate their subjective feelings of sexual arousal in response to sexual stimuli. That there are cultural differences in sexual attitudes suggests that social influences contribute to observed differences in sexual attitudes and behavior ... If religious teachings stigmatize sexuality in women, this may influence women's sexual attitudes and behaviors, and negatively bias their reported responses to sexual stimuli … The impact of socialized sexual attitudes and subjects' tendencies to match their perceived gender scripts to social expectations may explain much of the variability reported in the literature about reports of female sexual arousal. Women's subjective ratings of sexual arousal often do not match physiological measures of arousal.

If and how much social or biological factors affect our gendered behaviours is a continuation of the old argument about nature and nurture, but even that is a simplification, a dimorphic shaping of a multifaceted question. Nature and nurture are not 'opposites': they are interrelated influences that are sometimes difficult to tell apart, and which affect each other. Human bodies are confoundingly complicated: physiological, and especially neurological, states are affected profoundly by social and psychological factors. What we consider to be 'natural' varies wildly from culture to culture.

Binary thought doesn't offer freedom: it creates a series of mirrors masquerading as freedom, but which only replace one oppressive power structure with another, erasing the topologies of reality that refuse to fit its ideology.

As So Mayer suggests in their etymological essay series *Disturbing Words*, maybe we shouldn't think of gender as an abstract, intangible spectrum:

What if … we thought of gender as a landscape? Full of roughs and buttings-up, of pits and bumps and barks and falls. Tussocky underfoot. Very real, very uneven, very possible. Not landscape as vista, all sublime and far away. But underfoot or stick or wheel or hand, to be navigated with full attention. Full of alterations by generations of humans. In danger of privatisation, pollution, its specificities and granularities crumbling away under the force of human-made climate change.

In many places, gender has been blasted and monocultured, its disruptions and particularities paved over or bulldozed to grow rows and rows of identical GM stalks. Anything that doesn't serve capitalism's need for regularity gets called waste … and poisoned.

'Possible factors could be sociological, evolutionary, physiological, psychological, or most likely a combination.' Complex.

Reading into a self

Patriarchy. After all these years, after all this shouting, it still remains curiously invisible. Among its most grievous harms is how it distorts and destroys relationships between women: how it creates this deadly competition, in which every other woman is a rival; how it injects self-hatred, the internal abyss that is the result of being denied subjecthood. The inadmissible shame. The shaming.

Is it surprising that western women despise each other and, underneath, ourselves? For centuries, our foundational cultural texts have said, over and over again, that women are without worth. We have a role that defines us out of existence: as the possessions of men, we give birth and raise children. If we don't give birth, we have failed to fulfil our Destiny as Woman. If we do give birth, we can be nothing except a mother.

Motherhood turned me into a feminist. Even when I was

pregnant, I could ignore all the signals that indicated that I was an inferior human being. I could still pretend to myself that I could be equal (exceptional, not like 'the other women'; every woman who believes she is now equal actually believes she is not like other women). Once I had a baby, the veils were torn aside. I still remember, the sting undiminished, a male poet saying to my face: 'Well, that's the end of a promising young poet.' People felt they had the right to tell me I shouldn't be out in the street with a young baby; strangers rebuked me if the baby was crying or if they thought I wasn't looking after the baby well enough. I was suddenly an unperson — everything I was subsumed into a new role: 'mother'.

The shock of discovering that I was an unperson unravelled everything. The three months after the birth of my son was a strange, traumatic time. As if to mark my becoming a different person, I lost two stone. I discovered, perhaps for the first time, what it meant to love someone else, because the love I felt for my son was something against which I had no defences. The anaesthetised consciousness that had been me for the previous decade came to life, with a brutal joy. It was so hard, waking up. It remains so hard.

I felt that I was being remade, that I was evolving at a speed that was so dizzying that it made it impossible to recognise myself. I nearly killed myself proving the poet wrong, lying in bed writing poems in my head as I rocked a colicky baby on my chest. Words moved inside me like flames. This was when I, the *I* that I know as myself, began.

Before I had a baby, I barely thought about feminism. Again, it's hard to remember precisely, but I'm pretty sure

I regarded feminism as most women who reject it do: it was something that was irrelevant to my life, the province of the women in boiler suits who invaded a reading where I was present and militantly took over the mike to read poems about defacing the grave of Sylvia Plath. It was the realm of special pleading, unjustified victimhood.

I considered myself equal to men. I had put away *femininity*, without understanding that the femaleness of my body meant there was nowhere that I was ungendered. I hadn't yet learned that no matter what I did, no matter how hard I worked, no matter how smart I proved myself to be, I would never be equal.

I was raised in a house well stocked with books, the kind of books you find in a conventional middle-class house. From the age of about eight, I read everything I could get my hands on, which included every book in the house and, when I ran out of those, all the rejected books that were kept in a wardrobe in the shed. I was constantly hungry for more reading; I couldn't imagine having a single book in the house that I hadn't read.

No one took much notice of what I read; the only rebuke was that I read too much. In the seventies, addictive reading was considered in much the same way tabloids now regard video games, as a dangerously interior vice, and when my parents remembered, I was told to go outside and play.

My father read children's books all his life, just as I do: if he bought us a book as a gift, he was notorious for reading it himself first. So through the seventies and eighties, I read Lewis Carroll, Enid Blyton, the books of my father's childhood, Little Grey Rabbit, Geoffrey Willans and Ronald Searle's Nigel Molesworth books, the girls of St Trinian's, Alan Garner, Joan Aiken, J.R.R. Tolkien, Ursula K. Le Guin, A.A. Milne (including an odd collection of his plays). Much of my reading was way beyond my age: Thomas Hardy's *Tess of the D'Urbervilles*, Hammond Innes' *The Wreck of the Mary Deare*, Lawrence Durrell's *Alexandria Quartet*, anthologies of poetry that I sequestered as belonging particularly to me. All of Agatha Christie.

Reading was one thing: the profession of writing was another. To my family, professional writing was an oxymoron. My father didn't accept that writing was a proper occupation until I was forty, when I spent six months as a writer in residence at Cambridge University. It was the only thing that happened, aside from the publication of my fantasy books, that he genuinely respected. Before that, my insistence on writing was part of my being 'off the rails', a symptom of the fact that I hadn't 'settled down' and 'faced reality', part of my continual failure.

The months after the birth of my first child was the first time I really faced failure. It was bitter. I had already failed of my promise, I had already destroyed all my possibilities. That my poems would ever be published seemed utterly beyond the edges of possibility; it was likely that no one would ever read anything I wrote. In those sleepless nights, I began to list all the people I was, all the ways in which relationship defined me: mother, daughter, sister, poet, citizen, lover.

I watched a documentary on Herman Melville. *Moby-Dick;*

or, The Whale, his most famous book, was published in 1851 and was a commercial and critical failure. He never saw the more rhapsodic reviews; most critics followed the lead of *The Athenaeum*, which called it an 'ill-compounded mixture of romance and matter-of-fact'. By the time Melville died, a failed writer, it was out of print and his literary reputation was confined to a few European fans who sought him out when he was an old man.

The documentary didn't mention that Melville beat his wife, who managed his finances and through family connections found him the job as a customs officer that enabled him to earn a living, didn't mention that he was an alcoholic and a family tyrant. But even then, despite the fact that I still hadn't worked out that 'genius' is a profoundly gendered word, I was beginning to question the ideas that underlay my expectations of myself as a writer.

After watching the documentary, I asked myself if I would still write poems even if they would never be published, even if no one ever read them.

Yes. Yes, I would.

It was perhaps the most serious answer I ever gave myself.

Books saved my life; they woke me up. I started reading feminist texts. Audre Lorde, the great American poet, whose generosity and largeness of mind and spirit still inspires me. Betty Friedan, Luce Irigaray, Adrienne Rich, Marilyn French, Gloria Steinem, Robin Morgan, Simone de Beauvoir, Andrea Dworkin ... So many failed mentors. Alice Walker, who has turned into an anti-Semite, assured me that I could be a mother and a writer. Mary Daly and her separatist, wild-woman theorising and gyn/ecologies, who fascinated me with her totalising rivalry of patriarchy, who shocked me with her violent anti-maleness. Germaine Greer, who despised so many women, maybe all women, and yet whom I admired for her lawlessness.

I read hungrily, messily, without discipline, as I still do. I scarcely remember some of those books. I don't know how much I understood of what I read then, but what I did understand seared and changed me. It gave me the beginnings of a language.

I decided also to become well read in the European canon of patriarchal modernity. This was largely out of spite. As a young woman, I was routinely patronised by male poets, who wanted to fuck me and make me into their Muse. Even before I had babies, I was wary of Musedom: it was weird and embarrassing and insulting. Those poets were saying: you will never be my colleague. They were saying: you will never be my friend. (Women, they were saying to me, can't be friends — not with each other, and especially not with men.) I wanted to be the author of my own life. I wasn't interested in being someone else's helpmeet, someone else's inspiration. I didn't want anyone else writing me.

By my early twenties, I had read a lot of poems, but I hadn't taken much notice of who wrote them. I hadn't read biographies or histories or critical texts. As a child, I read what I found, in the anthologies we had at home, in the books I bought at jumble sales. T.S. Eliot and Lewis Carroll, Marianne

Moore and Henry Vaughan, Wallace Stevens and Stevie Smith. Later, I began to buy my own books, but although I had collections by Sylvia Plath and Ted Hughes, I didn't know they were married. Or that they even knew each other. I started to make connections, the critical constructions that allow you to put things together but that also so often end up obscuring the poetry itself in favour of things like significance, fame, and reputation (poets guard their reputations as fiercely as Victorian ladies).

Once I asked another (male) poet what modernism and postmodernism were. Instead of answering my question, he sneered at my ignorance. I decided, with a kind of stubborn fury, to teach myself. A friend of mine, also a poet, also a sole parent, was studying a course in postmodern poetics at Melbourne University, and she gave me her reading list. I ploughed through the whole thing with an increasing sense of vertigo — Lyotard, Jameson, Baudrillard — bewildered and lost in the unfamiliar language. (What did it mean that the bourgeois self didn't exist? I was a bourgeois self, I thought dizzily, and I existed. Or maybe not … ?) I persisted, until I began to understand the language, but because I was constructing myself, rather than pursuing an education, I only really persisted with texts that opened out the world for me. A lot of my readings remain failures. I was never taught to read properly.

I read religious texts: the Bible, the Upanishads, Judaic lore, the Apocrypha, the Sufi mystics, Teresa de Ávila, St John of the Cross, *The Cloud of Unknowing*. Poems, plays, novels, histories, philosophy. Philosophy both attracted and repelled me: some I devoured, some I never managed to read. I never got past page eleven of *Being and Time*, although I was fascinated by Heidegger's shorter essays, because they were about poetry. I remember the moment I put *Being and Time* aside: I felt smothered by the language, inarticulately suspicious of how terms like *quotidian* featured in his thinking. (It was not a surprise later to read about his Nazism, or how his critique of the rationalist west underpinned later Iranian Islamic revolutionaries Ahmad Fardid and Ali Shariati.) I couldn't even begin to read Lacan: something in the very texture of his language seemed to throw me out. Even the feminists urging me to read him couldn't get me through his prose: everywhere I felt an ugliness of misogyny, an erasure. I was placed as absence, as a hole. Un/w/hole.

I read Spinoza, Descartes, volumes of Freud's case histories and essays, Nietzsche. With writers like Nietzsche, the self I was as a reader wasn't an absence or an erasure. It was toxic and distorted, but at least it was present. There was an urge to freedom in many of these writings that excited me, that I encountered as doors opening.

But the more I read, the more I wondered about these great men, the men who imagined themselves behind sublime, intellectually swollen foreheads, the men who spoke of gestating great works, who spoke of being pregnant with thought, who heroicised the feminine in themselves while at the same time erasing it in actual women. Someone, somewhere, was taking care of their dinner, warming their beds, making their lives comfortable in countless small ways that they both demanded and despised.

I began to think about the things that are implicitly comprehended in the quotidian, which more and more I read as code for the *feminine*: the softness of arms that embrace rather than kill, the language of babies, the companionship of domesticity, the conversation over a table laden with food, the beauty of a natural world that is permitted merely to be instead of being possessed, the slow, gentle making of a good, embodied life. The touch of skin on skin that is not a metaphor for conquest, but acknowledgement; knowing as a negotiation of distance and intimacy and strangeness, knowing that is not a tool of ownership. The possibilities of love.

Again and again, in writings of so many kinds, I read how these, the quotidian, the everyday, the sphere of feminine domesticity, seduce and corrupt the masculine soul. Women are a necessary evil that must be confined because we are the vessel for the male progenitor, the incubator of his children who will continue his name and found his house. In abstract or in concrete terms, almost everything I read told me how the masculine soul is the intellectual, striving self that must pursue its fatality, sometimes towards God, sometimes towards victory over some abject or evil others. This is the self that must kill God not in order to free the world from God's shackles, but in order to become God himself. The feminine is rendered as bourgeois, and is drawn again and again as seductions, irrelevancies, distractions, and corruptions from purity, honour, authenticity — the hard, discrete self.

Woman creates life, and so is inferior. Man desires death, and so is superior: he transcends the mundane, branding his world with his superiority. But woman, having been set as inferior, is also ideal, perfect, sublimely beyond male perception: utterly legible, transparent to all male readings of her behaviour, but at the same time utterly strange in her profound triviality, the mysterious potency of her beauty.

It's difficult to negotiate these paradoxes, especially as a person signified as a woman. When you consider these claims next to the practical materiality of getting through life as a human being, they are patently nonsensical, the purest delusion. I, as a woman, have desires and needs as profound and contradictory as any man. I am neither innately superior nor inferior, no more mysterious or strange than any other human being, no less singular, no less private, no more nor less apt to comprehension, equally as capable of intellectual speculation.

Yet I am forced to go through life meaning both more and less than anything I actually am. I am forced to be a symbol of many things that I, personally, am not: 'Woman' is a sigil I carry everywhere with me, as inescapable as my own breasts. I can't rid myself of these symbols: they infect my entire embodied existence.

No wonder women learn to hate themselves. Our bodies determine everything we are allowed to be.

So much risible nonsense has been written to justify the inferiority of the feminine body. Camille Paglia's Freudian babble in her introduction to *Sexual Personae* is a notable example. 'The woundlike rawness of female genitals is a symbol of the unredeemability of chthonian nature,' she says. 'In aesthetic terms, female genitals are lurid in color, vagrant in contour, and architecturally incoherent. Male genitals, on the other hand, though they risk ludicrousness by their rubbery indecisiveness (a Sylvia Plath heroine memorably thinks of "turkey neck and turkey gizzards"), have a rational mathematical design, a syntax.'

I can never get over the sheer absurdity of this passage. Whenever I read it, I laugh. But at the same time, something inside me goes cold with recognition: here is the endgame of a self-confirming logic that has accreted over centuries, over millennia. A says a thing is so, and B argues further that it is so, and so on and so on through endless alphabets of thinkers, moving reality further and further away from the real, until this thing is so much *so*, so embedded in the real, that there is no undoing it.

Yet — how is it possible for anyone who has observed actual genitals of any kind to make such claims? What Paglia writes here literally makes no sense. (She is making claims about culture, but locating them in the specifics of the male and female bodies, as if biology alone is a determinant of how culture works.) It is impossible to argue such claims, because they are so nonsensical: they are arbitrary value judgements. Let a equal x.

Even so, I can't help pondering them. Both male and female genitals have the soft mucosity of mouths and lips, and those organs are on public display for our entire lives. Even though the latter act as entrances to the interiors of our bodies, they are seldom thought of as 'raw' or 'woundlike'. Both masculine and feminine genitals become engorged with the same rationality of desire. They both are excretory organs — or at least, the male organ is, because the male urethra passes both semen and urine, whereas the female urethra is totally separate from the vagina.

(As I write this, I find myself loathing the formal vocabularies we use for our genitals, which I am using for accuracy: they express little beyond the dry language of the medical report or anatomies, and hold no fondness. *Vagina* comes from the Latin for 'scabbard': it is a passive thing that merely holds a weapon, and its rhyme is the sword that goes inside it, and it is made to belong to a man. *Penis* derives from the Latin for 'tail', which is at least an organic thing, playful and harmless, part of the body. But as usual, I digress ...)

Both male and female genitals 'risk ludicrousness': a lot of comedy, and much of the pleasure of lovemaking, in fact depends on mutual delight in our ridiculous vulnerability.

Mainly, I wonder how it is possible, on the one hand, that female genitals are 'incoherent' while male genitals are 'rational'? Is Paglia really locating human consciousness in our genitals, so they can make 'arguments'?

Repression is, Paglia says, a necessary aspect of consciousness, because if we were aware of the reality of our bodies, it could 'drive us mad'. Quoting the Hungarian Freudian Sándor Ferenczi, she says:

'The periodic pulsations in feminine sexuality (puberty, the menses, pregnancies and parturitions, the climacterium) require a much more powerful repression on the woman's part than is necessary for the man.' In its argument with male society, feminism must suppress the monthly evidence of woman's domination by chthonian nature. Menstruation and childbirth are an affront to beauty and form. In aesthetic terms, they are spectacles of frightful squalor.

Even given Paglia's conscious provocations, the assumption underwriting this — the primordial disgust invoked by the functions of the female body — seems to me merely bizarre. (I feel no such visceral disgust, perhaps an error of my upbringing. I remember reading in a women's magazine about the scandal of Marilyn Monroe staining her bedsheets with menstrual blood, and feeling puzzled. It's just blood, a mess: that's all it is.) Either male and female bodies are equally disgusting, or they are equally not disgusting. We all share the bodily functions of eating, excreting, defecating, burping, farting, fucking. Our skin is a permeable organ, and we are all full of holes that let in light and air and sound and the chemicals that stimulate taste and smell. We are each, men, women, and others, as natural and unnatural as other human beings, subject to the squalor and disorderly order of nature.

The cultural repression of our embodied nature is central to Paglia's thesis. I don't in fact disagree with her argument that western culture, as she conceives it, is at once a rejection and a fetishisation of the natural. I was brought up on a farm, witness to animals eating each other, mating with each other, giving birth, eating, shitting, and dying. I too don't have a lot of time for the sentimentalisation and euphemism with which we are too apt to regard the natural world. But Paglia's revulsion, the prurient fascination that she names as decadence and fashions into expressions of shock, feels more like a symptom of pathology than a diagnosis.

We are all bodies: me writing this, you reading this. It seems absurd to loathe and despise our very existence, but this is what our culture has taught us to do. In particular, it has taught us to load the horror and loathing of our embodied existence onto the female body. Body horror in movies is all about disgust for the maternal, the slime and blood of childbirth that is transformed into a signifier of death.

The conventional argument for this is that our bodies remind us that we are finite, bound in time. They will rot in the earth or, more likely these days, will be burned. The delusion is that if we escape our bodies — if we abstract ourselves into, say, something like writing — we will become 'immortal' and transcend our own deaths. And for centuries, our culture has named mortality as female, and reserved immortality for men.

Weirdly, Paglia's argumentative genitals, coherent and incoherent, find an echo in a much later work by Naomi Wolf, *Vagina: A New Biography*. She writes, with the kind of supreme silliness known only to the obliviously entitled, about the 'brain–vagina connection' that she calls the 'female soul' or 'the Goddess'. The vagina is, she claims, the road to female transcendence, the source of a magical feminine consciousness and creativity that can only be sourced through the release of sexual pleasure. This vagina, and the power that goes with it, is very white, straight, and middle-class, and the pleasuring requires all kinds of male go-betweens, including a creepy yogi-type figure who knows how to release the inner goddess.

As Laurie Penny said in the *New Statesman*, 'Throughout *Vagina*, Wolf refers to something called the "Goddess", a sort of wibbly-wobbly divine feminine energy that can be woken by appropriately angled vaginal massage and a nice bunch of flowers, a strategy known, and I really wish I were making this up, as the "Goddess Array".' It's the kind of book you read with your eyebrows up, the kind of book that's tailored for a hugely publicised literary scandal that has the useful side effect of making feminism as silly as Paglia claims it is.

Vagina claims, as Paglia does in *Sexual Personae*, that our consciousness — nay, our whole being — is determined by the physiology of our genitals. I'm as attached to my genitals as any human being, but the only way I can be entirely a cunt is metaphorically.

Both of these books are symptomatic overcorrections to the profoundly gendered realities of western culture, polar but curiously similar responses to the repressions that both of them note. As a culture, we are so saturated in our gendered discourse it's impossible to see outside it, to conceive of any reality in which our genitals might be simply our genitals, and not one of the major means through which we order social power and cultural significance.

There are cultures that order things differently. But this is my culture.

Crisis

When I think of what happened between me and my sister, it all seems — it all *is* — so irredeemably trivial. There's no totalising trauma that explains everything, no single catastrophe or series of events that might give this narrative a shocking centre from which can radiate the desired paths of sorrow and expiation.

Compared with most people, we have been so very fortunate: there are the ordinary tragedies of a middle-class, white family, but they are not reinforced by the racism and classism that are the sorting tools of the empire. (Sexism, sure: I've encountered that, sometimes in ways that make me shake with rage. I recognise my own scars in those of other women. I recognise them in all my sisters, in my daughter, my mother, my friends, in contemporary accounts and histories. But those other structural injuries? No. They do not belong to us.)

I don't know how to explain the relentless, exhausting,

traumatic tedium that was the bare ground of our relationship. It continues to be a continual low-grade disaster that just keeps happening, over and over again. I have simply absented myself from the arena, but that hasn't stopped any of it happening.

It's tiny things that, grain by grain, silt up the vital rivers, until the entire landscape is a desert; the incessant feed of toxins, drip by drip by drip, that mount in the blood until the whole body convulses.

Sometimes something in me would revolt. It seemed to happen every couple of years. There would be some conflict or event, usually little different from business as usual, and suddenly I couldn't bear it anymore. I would try to protect myself, try to set boundaries. Until the past few years, they only lasted until next time.

There was, for example, that day, maybe a month before the 2003 invasion of Iraq, when she walked unannounced and uninvited, as she always did, into my house. I had been unexpectedly invited to Switzerland to speak at a symposium about Australian literature, and for that I had to write three hour-long lectures. Because I had no university education, I was kind of winging it, as I always wing it; I'd never attended a university lecture. I had a fortnight to read the books I needed and to write the essays. At the same time, someone asked me to coordinate the Australian part of the Poets Against the War protest, which meant calling out and collecting the poems and arranging for their physical delivery, in a kind of poetic petition, to the Australian Parliament. This was part of an international protest, and the poems all had to be delivered on the same day all around the world.

It was one of my flat-broke periods, which were always a bit weird for me because, as an artist, these were mixed up with strange privilege (that time I went to Perth to the opening of my first opera, and had to borrow money to pay for my kids' meals while I was away). I was flying to Bern, city of marionettes and Paul Klee, but we had zero cash.

The internet was different then, and things were harder to coordinate. The printer wasn't working and I couldn't afford to get it fixed, and I didn't have (don't have) a car. There was no money for printing out documents or for a courier. I was writing lectures in the morning and managing the other endless details of the Poets Against the War in the afternoon. I was getting through the week, with the help of friends, but the thread was getting tighter and tighter.

One of the essays I was writing was called 'Dystopian Visions of Australian Poetry'. Reading it again, I realise I have always been grappling with the same alienations:

> Australia's sense of inhuman space and extrahuman time, the legend of Terra Nullius written onto the map of Australian geography and law, has led to a largely unacknowledged nihilism which abides in much Australian culture: for example, a peculiar self anaesthetisation and relentless, empty materialism: and also our traditionally vexed relationship with the environment, which has most often been inscribed in terms of struggle and antagonism, or even hatred. It's a relationship which is full of

contradictions and different embattlements: for example, the first Green Party in the world was formed in Tasmania. It's important in this discussion to remember that Australia is one of the most urbanised countries on earth: we are a population concentrated along the coastline, looking out towards the sea rather than inwards to an emptiness which we cannot compute and so, like so much of our complex history, simply deny. In its place we put the romance of the Australian bushman, the rural 'battler', and a degraded idea of Aboriginality, tourist brochure images with which we coddle our four-wheel-driven urbanity; or conversely, we imagine ourselves as an entirely urban society. I think neither are true reflections and reflect rather a traumatic response, the neurosis of repetition which returns obsessively to a missed encounter with our environment, erecting in the place of the absent encounter a sentimentalised and dishonest image of ourselves.

My sister knew that I was under a lot of pressure, because I had told her. Later, I realised that was probably why she had chosen that particular time, sniffing blood in the water (I was always careful to hide weakness, looking back). She hadn't called to see if I had a moment, because she never did: I presume that was because I might say, no, please come another time, and she didn't want to give me the choice. But perhaps she also believed it was her entitlement, to just walk in, no matter what was happening, and demand my complete attention.

Without even a greeting, she sat across from me at the kitchen table where I was working and began to talk at me.

ALISON CROGGON

Today, she was — as she had been, almost every day, for months before, years before — in crisis. That day, the day she walked in, knocking to pieces the delicate balance of my day, she talked at me for two hours. She just kept talking as I sat, silent, on the other side of the table in the ugly brick-veneer rental I lived in then, with its orange cupboards and cracking squares of grey lino, and she retold the same complaints and grievances that she had been rehearsing for months, for years, continually reshaped into the same monologue of victimhood.

I can't recall what the problem was. Something to do with her ex-husband, or our mother, or our father, or her children. Maybe it was to do with all of them. I probably gave her the same advice I always gave her, and which she never acted on. I do remember what I felt like afterwards. It was as if I had been bludgeoned. When she left, I sat at the kitchen table, unable to move, as if every bit of vitality had been sucked out of me. My husband walked into the kitchen and asked if I was going to vomit, because my face was so white. I had nothing left. I felt completely erased.

I remember thinking, *I can't do this anymore. I can't. I just can't.*

I think it was the first time that I realised that I couldn't be the mother that she wanted, that I couldn't be the sister that she wanted, that I couldn't ever answer the needs that she laid out across the table, because they weren't needs, they were something else, some kind of assault that couldn't ever be countered or answered. I could turn myself inside out trying to fill that emptiness, and it would make no difference.

The neurosis of repetition which returns obsessively to a missed

74

encounter with our environment, erecting in the place of the absent encounter a sentimentalised and dishonest image of ourselves.

She was constantly in crisis. It was always the worst crisis — nobody else ever had crises as bad as she had. Other people's crises were always their own faults. It was my fault I was poor, it was my fault I had been a single mother, it was my fault I suffered domestic violence and fled my home, it was my fault I never was able to buy a house. These were all evidence of my extravagance, my lack of judgement, my loose morals, my selfishness. But if bad things happened to my sister, they were the fault of everybody else.

Sometimes we got into pointless arguments, when she'd tell me that I couldn't possibly understand what it was like for her, being a sole parent: and I would say, but yes I do, of course I do, you know that, I was on my own for years. And she would say, no, it was much worse for her, and finally I would say: listen, I was looking after our mentally ill sister when I was the sole parent of two children under three! When I couldn't cope with that, I was evicted from my house by police! I was so poor I didn't pay rent for a year! I ran away from my home with my three-month-old baby and two small children because my partner abused me! You know all this, because I stayed with you! How can you say that, when you own your house, when your children are almost adults? And we would actually brawl about it, in our ridiculous version of the oppression Olympics.

I always despised myself after those arguments.

I suppose what she meant was that, when things happened to me, they didn't hurt *her*. It is difficult to understand another's pain. Sometimes it's easier just to pretend that there's no pain at all.

I was beginning to understand that she didn't want this emptiness to be filled or answered. The Crisis wasn't a problem to be solved or even annealed, which is why she never took my or anybody else's advice. The current crisis merely prepared the ground for the next crisis; it was a perpetual motion of crisis, insoluble, immovable, with no beginning and no end. Her crisis was the most jealous of gods: there was no other crisis save hers. There was, always and only, the Crisis, into which she fed every activity of her life, to which she sacrificed all her relationships. She was, always, a victim — the victim — blessed and armoured by her victimhood, beyond all criticism.

Maybe — it's hard to remember — maybe that day I began to understand that we didn't have a relationship. I didn't know what we had. And maybe that was when I suspected that it wasn't simply that she was indifferent to my own situation when she decided to bludgeon me with her suffering, that my being under such stress was in fact the reason that she did it. But although this kind of thing happened again and again, although any stress or weakness was, over so many years, the signal for this kind of assault, I really didn't want to believe it.

I could forgive the perpetual crisis: it's only exhausting. What I couldn't forgive were the prerogatives that she thought went with the crisis, the lack of empathy that sat alongside her continual demands for my time and attention and compassion. I couldn't forgive the distortions and erasures that were necessary to bolster this victimhood, this status of untouchable specialness that entitled her to nothing less than everything. The way that what happened between us was never about a struggle, no matter how difficult, towards mutual understanding, but about who won.

I never understood what the prize was. Over the years, it just became clearer and clearer that everybody lost.

'[The] feedback between liar and lie-ee has immense psychological significance,' says English professor Colin Burrow, in a fascinating essay in the *London Review of Books*.

> It's the reason why, in fiction and in life, lies can have such a powerful effect. If they take us in it's because they work with our beliefs about what is likely to be true … the victim's prejudices and assumptions about what is likely to be true play a key role in determining the kinds of statement a liar can get away with. Lying is a social act that is crucially dependent on the beliefs of the person lied to, whom I will call the lie-ee. The words generally used to describe such a person — 'victim', 'gull', or the philosopher Sissela Bok's favoured term, 'dupe' — implicitly ascribe weakness to the deceived and deprive them of agency.

Was lying the problem? I never believed my sister's stories, because I knew they weren't true. In any case, they were always said *about* me, never *to* me. I simply didn't think they mattered. (On that, I was wrong.) They were, in any case, impossible to confront in any meaningful way.

Why did I put up with it for so many years? Was it because these stories confirmed what I secretly suspected to be true: that I am without worth, that I am a bad, selfish, vain person whose good acts are merely accidental, who is at best well meaning but is essentially destructive, essentially a failure?

Did it give me a way out?

After our breach, I began to trawl obsessively through forums in which people discuss narcissistic siblings. Many of the forum members are around my age, in their fifties. They say that they can't believe it has taken them so long to understand. I see the same frustrated detailing, the same trivialities that build and build into an intolerable burden. Some of them are completely broken by a lifetime of being manipulated and exploited, by the gaslighting and the guilt, by the shame they suddenly realise they shouldn't feel, but cannot exorcise.

There are long, endlessly dull stories of endlessly trivial conflicts. There is little that is dramatic — sometimes there is conflict over wills, about how the others were cheated out of houses or goods, or brutal treatment in moments of crisis — but mostly it's a war of attrition. Year after year after year of constantly shifting manipulations, of subtle belittling and small libels, that finally the writer can't stand anymore.

It's too familiar. This frustrated, clotted, tedious telling is what I'm doing now. Behind it is a suffocating feeling that no one will believe what I say, that my bad faith is so well established, so obvious, that nothing else can be visible. That saying this aloud is indeed solid proof of ill intention.

Luckily for me, I have never been in a position where my sister has real power over me. This is partly because I am the oldest sibling. (Maybe it's not simply luck, maybe it's also an inner wariness, maybe it's my own self-centredness ...) That same luck is also my weakness, because that's how my sister can claim that she's my victim. I'm not continually in crisis, so therefore I can't be a victim. (*The* victim, there can only be a single victim ...)

I used to think that my wincing away from complaint was pride. Now I wonder if it's shame.

I often had a sense that things didn't really happen to me. I don't doubt that there are many reasons for this, but I'm sure that part of what caused it was my sister's constant erasure of my experience. *Drip drip drip.* (No, to be fair, it wasn't only my sister's erasure: she was only ever a willing handmaiden for the competitive power plays of patriarchy ...) Part of me believed — believes? — that I don't really deserve the good that comes my way. Whatever I achieve, according to this narrative, is through luck or cunning or manipulativeness; it isn't because I worked hard and sometimes that work pays off. The other side of this story is that I always get through hard times because I am never really having a hard time in the first place. She was telling me all those years that I didn't really *suffer*. Not like she did. Nobody did.

The strange thing is that I believed her.

I can sometimes trace the seed of her miasmic narratives, but not always. For years she claimed, for instance, that I stole her boyfriends, that my husband and the father of my two oldest children were her boyfriends first, until I seduced them away from her. But neither of them were ever in a relationship with her. Perhaps she simply wanted them, and wanting them transformed over time into the idea that they really had been her boyfriends. When I finally confronted her, naming names, in an abortive attempt to — what? Clear the air? Tell the truth? How laughable that seems now — she changed the accusation.

Then the story was that I had slept with five of her boyfriends. I rack my brains, and I can't think who they were. I once slept with one of her ex-boyfriends, maybe a year or so after they broke up. Maybe not so nice, but I wasn't nice. Who were the others? She didn't name them. I don't believe they exist. I can hear her saying, 'You don't remember, because you slept with so many people you've forgotten.' But I haven't forgotten that much. Does it matter? No, it doesn't matter — all this was decades ago, when we were young and fucked up. But it ends up mattering. It's as if she wants to take my life, my biography, and claim it for her own. *They weren't your lovers, they were mine.*

Similarly, she accuses me of trying to steal her daughter from her. At first, I laugh, because the idea is so transparently risible: how is such a thing possible? If anything, I have been an absent aunt; I have never been intimate with my niece. This accusation arrives after one of the few private conversations I have ever had with her.

And then I think about how assiduously my sister has cultivated a relationship with my own daughter. It's one of the many family rules where it's okay for her but not for anyone else. When my daughter was a teenager, my sister hired her to tidy my niece's room or to tutor her. It was some pocket money, which was scarce in our house, so I never interfered, but it felt uncomfortably as if she were merely there to be a servant. I think about how my daughter became a substitute parent to my niece, emotionally responsible for her cousin in a way she should never have been, in a way that discomfortingly echoes my own position in the family. I think of the times when my sister outright claimed that she knew my own daughter better than I did, in order to suggest that my daughter was lying to me.

I resent, helplessly, how my daughter has borne this burden for all these years, for decades, how adept she had to become to be carefully neutral in all our sisterly conflicts. It's a purely family joke to call my daughter Switzerland.

Those stories about how, through her hard work, my sister gave me the breaks in my (so-called) career, which out of my ingratitude and selfishness I never acknowledged. The less we have to do with each other, the more fictional these become: she told my mother recently that she was responsible for getting me my first libretto commission. I have no idea what seeded that one, because she had nothing whatsoever to do with the chain of events that caused that to happen, not even remotely. Perhaps it's an expansion of that time when she 'got me an agent', which meant that she asked her neighbour, who then worked in publishing, if she knew of any, and passed on an address. There were kindnesses and favours, to be sure, that I had thought were part of a mutual exchange, part of the relationship I thought we had, but were instead listed on an invisible ledger that tallied up only debt. My sister in fact used the petty fame I was accruing as a young poet to bolster her claims to legitimacy: I and my friends were part of her 'extensive contacts in the arts industry'. My side of it was always erased; anything I offered and gave was simply rubbed off the ledger.

Sometimes — maybe more often than I knew — she just took. One of the worst fights we had was when she used my name, without my permission or knowledge, to wangle an appointment with a friend who was then an executive with a Melbourne arts company. He complained to me, nicely, that she had wasted his time, and I was mortified. But when I brought it up with her, she told me she had every right to do that, that I had no right to deny her, that this was how corporate business, about which I knew nothing, was done.

Then there are the outright conspiracies: the accusations that I was in league with her ex-husband, plotting against her, when in reality I scarcely knew him and didn't speak to him for years after their separation; that I 'interfered' in her relationship with her daughter in order to deliberately alienate her; and so on. The insistence that all my actions are vicious, that any action, even the most benign and transparent, is deeply malignant and damaging ... The way that she has always put the worst possible construction on anything I do, as if there were no barrier between suspicion and fact. The logic of malleus maleficarum, the hammer of the witches: any accusation is proof of crime.

All complicated by the mediations of others — who said what to whom, when? Who can keep track?

Triviality upon triviality. One small dishonesty here, one slightly warped story there, one ever-swelling exaggeration elsewhere. Nobody has the energy to challenge the details and so they mount up, until after years and years a whole populous mirage hangs in the air. The story changes when it is challenged, and the challenge itself becomes another crisis, another maelstrom of talking and talking and talking and talking, going over and over the same things in diminishing circles until nobody cares anymore what the real story is, because they're all so exhausted, because whatever was important in the first place has long been forgotten.

Sometimes, in nauseating moments of vertigo, I wonder if the things she claims about me might be somehow true. That some other being that looks like me, sounds like me, smells like me actually did all those things, plotted with those people, stole her lovers and her rights and her places and her achievements. A malicious doppelganger, who inhabits the same space I do and who works without my knowledge, whose every word is said in bad faith, whose every action is an attempt to destroy my sister.

There is no undoing it. This shifting miasma is the only continuity. Does she even know she's doing it? Surely she does: she couldn't so carefully edit the realities she tells to each person if she were not consciously curating them. Or maybe that's just the limit of my own imagination.

Maybe I could forgive even that, if it weren't for all the damage it causes. The relationships it poisons, the exhaustion and depression that it sows. The traumas that it reproduces, over and over again, in herself, in others.

Once I thought that maybe if she started succeeding at something, if maybe she stopped feeling insecure, it would give her a place to consider and to think, to change her behaviour. But it didn't.

(It's hard to write this. Asserting my own claims is somehow cringe-making. One doesn't assert these claims, one doesn't boast of one's own generosities, because it cancels them out; it erases them as exactly as she does, sucking them of any life, as if one's own generosities were important or exceptional; it takes these small actions out of the easy play of being in the world, so they are no longer part of give and take, as if they were only take. I want to take this shame and make it into something else, a tool, a door, a window, a seed, a flowering, a libation, an offering to the wounded earth ...)

It took me five decades to give up, to realise that nothing would ever change.

I can't but recognise that this behaviour must emerge from some terrible pain, even if the source has been long forgotten. My sister has all the foundations for a wonderful life. She has been given support — so much support — in situations in which I had none. She will never acknowledge these privileges; she will use them as proof of her superiority over me, but they will never mitigate her essential victimhood.

But all the same, at a safe distance, I pity her. I don't feel pity close up, though. I know that lure too well; I am so familiar with the seduction of compassion. Pity is what she wants, because it is a kind of absolution, a strange permission. But she's drawn me into that dark gravity and burned me too often.

I see the wound that she suffered, because it's my wound too. I thought she knew that. That she denies this common wound — that she claims, instead, that I am the knife, the bludgeon, unfeeling, insensate, solely destructive — feels like the most profound, the most bitter betrayal.

All her life she has shouted out of this wound, but always she turned away from it. She has sacrificed everything so she need never look at it. Her joy, her possibility, her generosity, her life.

I don't know how to help her. I have never known how. Somehow helping her became my responsibility. There's still a part of me that feels guilty for being unable to solve anything, because it's true, I didn't solve anything at all.

Mortality

It's five years after that final letter from my sister. 2020.

I wonder what will happen if I get sick, or if my sister gets sick. I know for sure that if I become ill, I don't want her anywhere near me. If I get sick, everyone will be dealing with her crisis as well as whatever else is going on, just as any family emergency is always inevitably a time when her crisis, put on its mettle, flowers histrionically into everybody else's problem. She is always exhausting; she always sucks up all the energy that should be spent dealing with the emergency itself.

But if she gets ill? What then?

I deeply, profoundly, don't want my sister to get seriously ill, because I don't believe I can speak to her, even then, even in the extremity. I begin to realise that it's not about forgiveness. It's not about that at all. Forgiveness is kind of irrelevant.

If it were simply about forgiveness, I could make some kind of choice.

I hear the wail in my mind when I even think about such a rapprochement: *I can't. I just can't.* How small, how petty, how selfish is that? I like to think I am a good person. My vanity is hurt when I find that I am less than empathic, less than just, less than a decent human being. But I'm not a good person. Not in any abstract, saintly sense.

I don't wish my sister any harm, and not only for selfish reasons, but I cannot contemplate any kind of intimate contact with her. I fear the compassionate impulse that would make me do that, the impulse to set myself aside that has always put me back into the same old prison. Her suffering must always be much greater than the suffering of others — but what if it actually is? What then?

No, I couldn't bear it.

What kind of person reacts like that? What sort of person is cruel enough to write it down?

Some kind of monster.

Me, it seems.

The pattern

Here we are, raised in a tiny pocket of this gigantic project, the genocidal con job that was the British Empire.

The connections aren't simple to trace, even though they are pervasive. They're invisible but palpable, like the air that is insensibly filling with carbon dioxide, slowly at first, but now faster and faster, turning up the heat on the tiny, fragile bell jar that is our planet. I can step back and see the effects; I can see the damage that is written on us. But cause and effect? They are skewed, slant, indirect, multiple.

The logic of it. I feel it in my being, this habit of mind we were raised with, the thoughts that close and direct perception, that keep us from the real. It's the double bind that proves to women that they are inferior to men, that proves to brown and Black people that they are inferior to white people. It's the logic of colonialism, a kind of deadly algorithm in which the larger patterns are reproduced in ever smaller iterations ad infinitum.

I stare at the beautiful, hypnotic images of Mandelbrot fractals, images generated by algorithms in sequences that I don't understand. Some animations continually increase the magnification, leading the eye into a dizzying abyss, down into the same, and then the same again and the same again. All the way in, from Clive of India through newspaper reports to taunts at school to the primordial quarrels of our splintered, alienated middle-class British Australian family.

But we aren't mathematics; or if we are, our relationships are ruled by variables that are beyond any present computation. a doesn't equal x. The debacle that is our sisterhood isn't a simple mirror of what our family did to the people they brutalised. It's not that I'm enlightened and decolonised and she is endarkened and still colonised. (Again, those binaries.) Who I am is so deeply conditioned by the culture in which I was raised that I don't believe that I will ever escape it: I am a painful work in progress, apt to failure. I can only, as I once heard said kindly of an acquaintance, do my best. And the truth is that often my best isn't very good.

We are both the product of a machine that has spent centuries concealing its violence, that pours countless resources into disguising its greed for resources and power as an exercise in human progress. And I don't doubt that we both find ourselves bewildered in its aftermath. The question we both have to face is whether we will continue the lie that divides the world along binary axes — good/bad, men/women, white/black, right/wrong, guilty/innocent. To protect those binaries, we do violence to ourselves and to each other. It's profoundly infected our relationship: in order for her to be good, I have to be bad; in order for her to be right, I have to be wrong.

For so many years I thought there was a middle way. For so many years I thought that we merely misunderstood each other, that if we could only speak clearly then we would begin to understand, to negotiate each other's complexities. When she hurt or embarrassed me, we all laughed it off as her famous tactlessness. And maybe, once upon a time, it was no more than carelessness.

We *were* careless, of ourselves and of each other. We didn't know how to care; we just assumed that we did. We were siblings fighting each other for attention, and there was never enough attention, because parents are only human, because parents are sometimes absent, because parents sometimes let us down. Sisters together, negotiating ideas of womanhood that we barely understood. Sisters who only knew each other and ourselves as the people we assumed we were, unthinkingly suspended in the cosmos that we were born into, that was already broken, that we thought was the shape of the whole world because it was the only world we knew.

There was a time when our relationship wasn't beyond repair. I'm sure this is true. Or maybe I'm unwilling to accept that this was determined from the beginning, that once the pattern was set (and the pattern was there before we were born) and once the damage occurred (and the damage happened when we were too young to do anything about it) everything else was inevitable.

She knows so little about me. She barely knows me at all. But I have listened to her for years, all those decades until I stopped pretending that we had a conversation. It's so hard to trace when it tipped. Change happens so insensibly, so slowly, and suddenly you are standing on a burning planet, watching the birds fall dead out of the sky.

I have words. From the forums, the pop-psychology articles. I've used some already. It helps a little, but also it doesn't. It explains nothing. It just gives me a few words that, in the way of words, are as imprisoning as they are illuminating. They don't explain things in the ways I need them to be explained. I need to comprehend how I too am part of this pattern, I need to understand the shapes of our common brutalisation, I need to see how our differences are enmeshed in much wider social pathologies.

I need to understand in this larger way so I can unpick the minutiae of my own psyche. I need to understand my own unhappiness and culpability. I need to know how not to reproduce this pattern, how to break it. I know that if I don't learn how to see these things, I can't properly perceive my own joy.

There is much in my life that is joyous, so many people and things that bring grace and beauty and delight. This writing isn't about joy, but joy comprehends everything that matters. Everything.

Scandal

It's spring in Melbourne. The weather is uneasy, shifting between warm, almost tropical showers, unseasonable heat, and strong winds that make the cats skittish — they flick their ears and tails and yowl at us as if the weather is our fault. We live on a peninsula, and the front door of this old rented weatherboard house is oriented towards the prevailing wind. It makes the house vocal: draughts whistle through the ill-fitting windows, sing through hidden holes.

It's two and a half years since I last spoke to my sister. It's almost exactly a year after *The New York Times*' revelations about Harvey Weinstein, a year after the #MeToo tsunami broke over social media, those weeks when I was scrolling through a solid wall of #MeToo on my Facebook and Twitter feeds. The internet is a trauma machine, recording and reproducing millions of psychic wounds. All the hidden flaws in the self are singing their pain.

People say, 'triggering'. #MeToo is, in the proper sense of the word: it brings up memories I had forgotten or, more properly, sent unexamined to the back of my mind. More memories. I hadn't realised there were so many. All the small, insidious incidents that on their own can be brushed off but which, small stroke after small stroke, add up to ... what? A deformation of the self, I guess. At that point, I realised I am in mourning for who I might have been if I hadn't been reshaped by all these tiny cuts.

I have never been able to look at espaliered plants without feeling a strange empathy. When a fruit tree is espaliered, it is transformed from a three-dimensional plant into two dimensions. A careful regime of pruning and pinning directs the growth of a tree's branches so they are wired flat against a wall, each branch stretched out horizontally in pairs. It is a neat, obedient tree that neatly and obediently offers its fruits, without any messy branches singing in the wind. It has its own beauty: the man-made beauty that makes a wall flower, the ingenuity that redirects growth into the desired, truncated shape. It cannot reach for the sun in its own way.

More than a decade before it went viral, the #MeToo movement was founded by a Black woman, Tarana Burke, as a way of helping survivors of sexual violence in low-wealth Black communities in the United States. It's now become a shorthand for so many things, many of them far removed from the community-based, grassroots approach to healing advocated by Burke. I watched as it became a lightning rod for anger, I watched the inevitable backlash gather force, I watched as it was turned into a weapon and used against women by men. I've watched it turn into a scandal.

The oldest definition the Merriam-Webster dictionary gives of scandal is:

> 5a: discredit brought upon religion by unseemly conduct in a religious person
>
> b: conduct that causes or encourages a lapse of faith or of religious obedience in another

It first appeared in Middle English, so the Oxford dictionary tells me, in its sense of 'discredit to religion (by the reprehensible behaviour of a religious person)', from Old French scandale, from ecclesiastical Latin scandalum 'cause of offence', from Greek skandalon 'snare, stumbling block'.

Is patriarchy a religion? (Is the Pope Catholic?)

Certainly there is conduct that has caused and encouraged a lapse of faith and obedience in all the (an)others.

A year after the Weinstein case, a celebrity defamation trial is in the news. I am following the Rush trial obsessively: I read every news report, I follow the hashtags on social media, I scan all the documents the Federal Court has made available because of the public interest in the case. My interest is partly professional: I have written about theatre for years, and when the Weinstein reports came out in the news, I conducted my own investigation into sexual harassment in Australian performance. I am also writing a long background piece about this particular trial.

It is, like everything, complicated. On the one hand, the newspaper that is being sued deserves to lose the case, because the article at issue is a lazy, salacious piece of shoddy reporting, the worst kind of predatory journalism. The woman at the centre of the allegations has been pulled into the maelstrom against her will; she never intended any of it to go public. I know her by reputation as well as through watching her on stage; she is widely respected by her colleagues. At the time, I had never met her.

My interest is also personal. My anger on behalf of the young woman who is standing up in court is also an anger for myself. For all my younger selves. I see her refusing the poison cloak of shame that is thrown over her involuntary nakedness. I don't doubt the shame burns.

There are so many things that cannot be said. The scandal. The snare. The stumbling block.

Trials are no place to determine truths. They determine probability. 'Beyond reasonable doubt'. 'Standard of proof'. 'A preponderance of evidence'. In the oral adversarial trial, the standard under common law, the arts of persuasion are paramount.

In both the man and the woman I see the shame of patriarchy, burning.

I see it in my sister too. I see it in me. In all of us.

As soon as we are in the midst of accusation and counteraccusation, the weighing of one set of evidence against another, we place ourselves before the judge.

The judge is old. He has white hair and, like a priest, he wears a robe that gives him the sacred mantle of androgyny, permitting him authority over both male and female experience. Like Tiresias, he is still, crucially, a man, just as the masculine pronoun embraces (once embraced) all sexes.

The judge determines who is heard and who is not. He divides the sheep from the goats, the good from the bad. He is the kind father, the stern father, the punishing father, the merciful father. He leans forward to make a joke, and the court erupts in laughter: the laughter is relief, that in the midst of such serious business, the business of life and death, of imprisonment and release, of guilt and innocence, we have such a small and light thing as a joke. It makes all these processes so much more human.

Even when we are not in court, the judge persists. He insinuates himself into every gesture, every thought. Here I am, sneaking into his robes, soberly discussing rights and wrongs, clarifying ambiguities, distinguishing between this and that, here and there, her and me, them and the others. Here I am, before the bench, my head bowed in shame, as he adumbrates my long history of convictions and wrongdoing, pointing out my grammatical errors and ethical shabbiness. He points his gavel towards these letters I am typing right now and bangs the bench and shouts: 'Contempt!'

Who am I to judge? we say, when we find ourselves unable to decide. We wash our hands and throw the question open to another authority.

I want to move out of court. I want to break down the

walls of the trial. I want a more generous means of measurement and consideration.

Behind the judge, there is always another judge. It's judges all the way up, until we reach God, seated in honour on his throne.

According to St John of Patmos, who saw it in a vision, God's throne room is pretty whack. I could never resist the rolling cadences of the King James Bible, even in all my fierce atheism as a child, even despite the despairing banality with which I associated the very word 'Christian', which for me summoned an image of something deathly, a washed-out illustration from a children's book of Bible stories.

Revelation, which for so many Christian people, some of them running governments, seems to be the text of our times. Before John describes the end of the world, with the four horsemen of the apocalypse and the seven seals and falling stars and giant locusts, he tells us about the Throne of God.

And before the throne there was a sea of glass like unto crystal: and in the midst of the throne, and round about the throne, were four beasts full of eyes before and behind. And the first beast was like a lion, and the second beast like a calf, and the third beast had a face as a man, and the fourth beast was like a flying eagle. And the four beasts had each of them six wings about him; and they were full of eyes within: and they rest not day and night, saying, Holy, holy, holy, Lord God Almighty, which was, and is, and is to come.

As well as all the beasts singing *Holy, holy, holy* in the midst of the throne and round about it, there's *lightnings and thunderings and voices* proceeding out of the throne. It's not clear whether the lightnings, thunderings, et al. are actually God or some kind of throne function. So this God is a thunder god, cousin to Zeus, Jupiter, Iškur, who is also known as Haddad, also known as Adad, also known as Rammanu, the Thunderer.

And he that sat was to look upon like a jasper and a sardine stone: and there was a rainbow round about the throne, in sight like unto an emerald. A sardine stone has nothing to do with fish: it means sard, a carnelian, brownish-red. Jasper may be red, green, yellow, or brown, or occasionally blue. I imagine a chunky, still, ruddy man. John doesn't say how big he is, but I presume he's impressively large, with animals full of eyes on his lap or squeezed up behind him on the throne, perhaps how the cat squeezes in behind me when I'm writing at my desk.

And round about the throne were four and twenty seats: and upon the seats I saw four and twenty elders sitting, clothed in white raiment; and they had on their heads crowns of gold. Four and twenty elders, the heads of the families of the twenty-four priestly courses who, in Chronicles, King David appointed to represent the priesthood. *And there were seven lamps of fire burning before the throne, which are the seven Spirits of God.*

In some interpretations, the Seven Spirits of God are the seven churches of Asia. Or they are dynameis, exalted spiritual beings like the angels, but not actually angels. Or they may be actual angels, for seven angels are named in the Book of Daniel. Or perhaps they are the seven archangels described in the Book of Tobit, when Raphael reveals himself, saying, 'I am Raphael, one of the seven holy angels, which present the prayers of the saints, and which go in and out before the glory of the Holy One.'

And when those beasts give glory and honour and thanks to him that sat on the throne, who liveth for ever and ever,

The four and twenty elders fall down before him that sat on the throne, and worship him that liveth for ever and ever, and cast their crowns before the throne, saying,

Thou art worthy, O Lord, to receive glory and honour and power: for thou hast created all things, and for thy pleasure they are and were created.

For thy pleasure they are and were created.

Patriarchy, all the way up.

Angels have no sex, but in the English Bible they read as masculine. There aren't many feminine aspects of God, but women can't be kept out altogether. Rabbinic texts talk about the Shekhinah, the dwelling of God. I feel a certain fondness for the Shekhinah, because the writings about it exhort a man to make love to his wife when he returns home after an absence, and stipulate that it is very important that the man gives the woman pleasure.

Sophia, wisdom, is a feminine aspect of God in both Judaic and Christian traditions. Solomon discusses *sophia* in the Proverbs. 'Say unto wisdom, Thou art my sister; and call understanding thy kinswoman,' he says, 'that they may keep thee from the strange woman, from the stranger which flattereth with her words.'

The 'strange woman' is very dangerous. Solomon goes on

to describe a foolish youth who wanders heedlessly into the twilight, the perilous time that is neither night nor day, and from there ventures on into the 'black and dark' night, where he meets a woman dressed as a harlot. She is 'subtil of heart', 'loud and stubborn', and 'her feet abide not in her house'. She catches and kisses this youth, and 'with an impudent face' she promises him a bed of fine Egyptian linen perfumed with myrrh, aloes, and cinnamon.

The subtil, dangerous knowledge of the unimprisoned woman is, naturally, fatal: the youth follows her as an ox to the slaughter 'till a dart strike through his liver'. Indeed, 'many strong men have been slain by her. Her house is the way to hell, going down to the chambers of death.'

In Proverbs 8, Solomon says that *sophia*, the woman whose feet abideth in the house, is better than rubies or silver or gold. It is *sophia* that anoints the authority of man. Wisdom, Solomon says, is how kings reign and princes decree justice: 'By me princes rule, and nobles, even all the judges of the earth.' And even though wisdom is better than rubies, or gold, or silver, it also guarantees that you have them all. Those who legislate with wisdom are prosperous and their treasuries are full. Which is handy.

Sometimes, in early gnostic Christianity, Sophia was twinned with Christ. But eventually she was swallowed by the Logos, the word of John, the Word of God that becomes flesh in the person of Jesus Christ. *In the beginning was the Word, and the Word was with God, and the Word was God.*

For me, the word was the beginning of consciousness. The word was how I began to explain myself to myself, beginning the conscious and unconscious building of everything I know to be me. It is where I began and where I constantly return.

Let a equal x. Let the Word equal God.

What if the equation is wrong, right back in the beginning?

(Of course the equation is wrong.)

I am a woman whose feet abide in the house much of the time. I miss my home when I'm away from it, and I like being here, among all the things that have accumulated over a lifetime: notebooks and libraries; the Georgian silver jug that my grandmother left me; gifts from my children; the little pewter pig my sister gave me once, long ago, with clouds inscribed on its shoulders; photographs; the little brass statues of Ganesh, god of story and of overcoming obstacles, whom I think of as my guides when I sit here, in front of a screen, writing down these words that I hope, one day, someone else will read with interest and pleasure and, perhaps, recognition.

I have never been able to escape the sneaking thought that, even as I abide, I am a blasphemy. Solomon wasn't speaking to me when he made his Proverbs: he was speaking to the men who would uphold his laws or break them, the men who might be seduced unto their death by the harlot with the impudent smile, the men who must keep the women orderly in their houses, the men who must reign and judge, listening to the wisdom that is passed down from God the father to God the son.

Sophia was silenced because the presence even of such a womanly unbody as Wisdom is too compromising, too close to the harlot. If a woman is to be holy, she must be desexed, as Mary was — lifted to an impossible chastity, which renders her as a passive receptacle that adds nothing to the genesis of godliness. The active wisdom of God, the Word, must be passed from the father to the son — not, as the patriarch's inheritance, through a child begat through the hollow vessel of a woman's body — but through the visions of the son of a fisherman called Zebedee, the visions of a man who with his brother James was called the 'son of thunder' and who supposedly died in Ephesus and was buried in a sacerdotal plate, a man who wandered through the desert and in his fiery visions saw the Throne of God and the seven lamps and twenty-four elders, the sea of crystal and the beasts full of eyes, a man who said he heard God thundering from his throne and who described the end of the world.

I am a woman who abideth in the house but who walks in the twilight, neither one thing nor another, loud and stubborn and impudent, stealing the word for my own.

Wrong in the very beginning.

Territories

'Each mode of power,' writes the Nigerian feminist Bibi Bakare-Yusuf, 'is like a thread that creates a pattern of significance only when woven together with all the other threads that combine in a specific situation (the family, the work-place, the city, the culture, and so on).'

I pull on one thread, then on another. There are so many threads, and each of them is so entangled, so contingent on each moment. Power, like art, only exists in its activation, and it is activated in so many directions. Its vectors change in every moment, class, race, sex, sexuality, ability, age. Now this, now that, each relative to each other; now I have power, in the next moment I have a little, in the next, none at all. All of us parse these things in so many ways in every moment of each of our lives.

Word-wrangling is my defining ability. As a journalist, I found being interviewed deeply alarming: it was, as I knew well, placing myself at the mercy of another's framing. Sometimes it was a purely professional alarm at seeing first-hand how others do their work: there was the woman who interviewed me by walking around a park and asking me a series of questions, neither writing down nor recording my answers, and who then printed what were supposedly my (mortifyingly inane) answers between quotation marks, as if I had actually said such things.

I aspire towards accuracy. I hate making mistakes; it hurts my pride. It doesn't mean that I'm never wrong: in fact, despite all my efforts, error follows me whatever I do. Like all writers, I have the power of being able to misrepresent, inadvertently or maliciously. I can't pretend to any kind of objectivity, and honesty compels me to admit that it is impossible not to misrepresent others, even in the best of circumstances. And these are not the best of circumstances. To be perceived by another is to be misrepresented. It's only a matter of degree.

There is no point in pretending that any writing is wholly disinterested. I can only write from my own subjectivity, which is conditioned and circumscribed by whatever it is I am capable of perceiving. Am I misrepresenting my sister? Perhaps more accurately: am I representing her at all? What right do I have to do so, in any case?

At base, my argument with her is her claim to objectivity, her claim that she speaks the Truth, that of us two, she is the only one who sees and tells the Truth. It's the obverse of her accusation that I am deceitful. But what have I to put against that except my own competing Truth? It feels so futile.

Our entire argument is about representation. When I

respond to the painful and distressing image she presents of me, this in turn misrepresents *her*. When I say that I'm not the things she says I am, this does something fundamental to *her*.

If I am not the monster she claims I am, the foundational logic dictates that she must be the monster. I am resisting this diagnosis. Binaries again, flipping this way, that way — but the problem always remains the same shape.

In between us lies a primordial trauma that can be neither erased nor named, that is neither remembered nor forgotten. But I think this goes far beyond us. We were born into patterns that shaped who we are, that shaped our parents and their parents before them. The damage was handed down, generation to generation, a damage that was understood and reproduced as privilege.

I was born in 1962. The Cuban Missile Crisis, a thirteen-day standoff between Russia and the United States that brought the world to the brink of nuclear catastrophe, occurred when I was less than a month old. I remember my mother telling me once of her fear when she brought babies into this world. She didn't mention the Cuban Missile Crisis, and it was only when I grew up and put the dates together that I realised that she must have been thinking about that terror.

Her father fought in the trenches of the Somme. I remember him talking about trying to match the different limbs of corpses, trying to work out which bit belonged to which body. He spoke of it lightly, as if it were a curious and funny story. Perhaps there was no other way to speak of such horrors to a small child.

My mother was a child of World War II. She remembers crouching in bomb shelters during air raids, remembers houses being bombed. It was her oldest brother, Tiny, who died on the HMS Hood, then the flagship of the British fleet, on 24 May 1941 during a battle with a German fleet in the Denmark Strait, a body of water between Greenland and Iceland. After its ammunition exploded and tore the ship apart, it sank in three minutes with 1,418 men.

After the war, the locus of power in the west moved from Britain to the United States: the sceptred isle owed a war debt of twenty-one billion pounds, a debt it only paid off finally in 2006. England dwindled, feeding itself on dreams of imperial exception that every decade became more and more deluded, until at last it became the ultimate petty clusterfuck of Brexit, the nation staring across the Atlantic in envy at the vicious, bloated delusion that is the empire of the United States.

Australia is still a colony. Our head of state is still the Queen of England. I am part of the British diaspora, which is considered to be qualitatively different because the British are not called immigrants but expatriates. Outside the fatherland.

I'm making a map. Another map. I like making maps, especially imaginary ones: it's another tendency of which I need to be suspicious. What do I need this map for? Is it a sign of ownership, or maybe a demonstration of relationship, or is it a means of navigation through a dark and difficult landscape? And there are so many possible maps, each of them different from the others, one overlaying the other: the family as an empire in miniature, tracing a genealogy through imperial geographies; the psychological map that is a topology of contested territories; the map as a cosmos, as an imaginary landscape of myths … (All maps reveal mythologies: some more overtly than others.)

The oldest maps of all are Aboriginal star maps, which were used to navigate their extensive trade and ceremonial routes around pre-colonial Australia, and which were passed from one to another through song. These seem the most beautiful of all — stars, singing, and walking — but I can't use that kind of map, it's not in my language, not my tradition.

I think of the Imago Mundi, the images of the cosmos that Romanian historian Mircea Eliade says are fundamental to religious belief, a way of creating order amid chaos. In the Imago Mundi, the world spreads out from the centre. A famous example is inscribed on a Babylonian clay tablet in around 600 BCE. It was discovered (pillaged) in the late 1800s in Sippar, Iraq, and is now part of the collection at the British Museum. It's an abstraction in the shape of a seven-pointed star, with notations in cuneiform. The middle of the star is circular, and in it are marked important cities and peoples, as well as geographical formations such as mountains and marshes and the Euphrates. Babylon is not quite in the centre: the centre is south of where Babylon is marked, and is probably Nippur, a city considered sacred because it housed the shrine of Enlil, God of the Winds. The empires of Persia and Egypt, which were known at the time, are not shown.

The landmass is surrounded by two concentric circles that are named 'bitter water' or 'salt water', the ocean that surrounds the world. And from the ocean stretch seven rays that represent islands that connect heaven and earth. Two are missing, because the tablet is broken. The islands are called 'beyond the flight of birds', 'the light is brighter than sunset or stars', 'the sun is hidden, nothing can be seen', 'here lives a horned bull that attacks the stranger', and 'place of the rising sun'.

In the Imago Mundus of my childhood, the centre of the circle is the nuclear family: me and my two sisters, my mother and father. Around us, in different positions but at a distance, stand our ancestors: on one side the Croggons, on the other the Rowes, grandparents first and biggest, and then aunts and uncles and great-aunts and -uncles. The first cousins are assembled in various orders of legibility, according to whom I remember best (the cousins I knew and played with in the three years we lived in England. There are some, who lived in the US, whom I mostly remember from photographs).

A wayward crack runs through the middle, and the tablet itself is broken, which means that much of the text is obscured. Around us is a circle of bitter tears, and from that radiates several spokes that cannot be counted, representing the bridges that once ran between heaven and earth, a unity that has now vanished. At least two are lost forever.

It's so very difficult to demarcate the self, to work out what has been inherited, what has been made, whether decisions we make originate from inner inclination or are the result of outside forces. Trying to work out who one is within the structure of a particular family is profoundly difficult, even for an adult. For us children, it was impossible. The family, perhaps our family more than others because of its isolation, created a totalising reality that determined everything about who we were. It was impossible to imagine ourselves outside its laws.

The fault lines through my parents' marriage were complicated, but worked their way through two major territories of class: the protestant materialist, like my father's family, and the romantic aristocratic, like my mother's. To be an artist was also to be aristocratic, whereas the protestant materialist was middle-class — decadent and irresponsible versus respectable and reliable, interesting versus dull, masculine versus feminine. These territories were marked out by both our parents, who assigned them different values, which became more polarised as their marriage deteriorated: what was a sin to my father was for my mother a virtue, and vice versa. These categories shaped our assumptions about who we were, and indelibly marked the relationship between us.

It fucked both of us up.

Three is the magic number, the step that follows from singularity and duality. It is the beginning of complexity in mathematics, the suddenly miraculous strength of the triangle in engineering. The three Fates, trading their one tooth and their one eye. The Graces. The Holy Trinity, the symbol of divine perfection. The triple-aspected Goddess, maiden, mother, crone. The three trees of faery, oak, ash, and thorn. The three spheres of the angels, each divided into three different kinds of angels. There are so many threes.

There were always three of us. Three sisters: our very own Olga, Masha, and Irina, or Goneril and Regan and Cordelia, or Charlotte and Emily and Anne. Three little pigs hiding from the wolf in our different houses, invisibly bound to our private, enmeshed world. But as in a geometric animation, the sides of the triangle fell apart and whirled off into singularity. We are no longer three: we are one and one and one.

How did it come to this? Were we the Ugly Sisters, quarrelsome, spiteful, and rivalrous, chopping off our toes to fit into the glass shoe? But if we were, who was Cinderella? Was she the possibility we never managed to reach, the real princess who went to the ball in her pumpkin carriage?

Perhaps none of these narratives were us at all. Perhaps we never comprehended our own story, so tightly wound as we were in the myths that defined us, glamours that confused the world as it is with the world as we wanted it to be. Or more likely, the world as we feared it might be.

We three made this world together, this encapsulation of sisterhood through which we defined ourselves and each other, for good and for ill. And now I stand alone in its rubble, staring out at a strange land beyond the walls that always enclosed me but that I only ever perceived dimly. How do I begin to understand?

My only tool is language. It's the only tool I ever had. And this uncertain medium sometimes seems like the source of all our misunderstandings, the will-o'-the-wisp that dances over the bare Cornish moors that haunt our childhoods, where skulls of sheep and wild ponies gleam whitely in the darkness.

In the mythology our family created in Australia, on the other side of the world from cousins and aunts and uncles and grandparents, we became our whole universe, self-referential and suffocating.

I genuinely don't know if it would have been more suffocating to have been raised in England, under the everyday weight of wider family expectations and traditions: it would have been a different kind of pressure, perhaps more insidious, or perhaps, being present, less so. Living in Australia might have given us a certain kind of freedom, a certain kind of access to choices that, as girls, we might not have had otherwise; or perhaps it fractured my sense of myself in ways that made it hard for me to make choices. Who might I have been if we had lived in England?

Sometimes I think that without the kind of dislocation that marks my life as a migrant, I might have turned into a person I would hate, insufferably without questions. Or maybe I was always going to be the kind of person I am now, only I might have wasted much less time trying to put myself together. It's impossible to know; I know these speculations are useless. I only have the life I have. But there are so many ways my life might have been different. What if my father had decided to make a life in South Africa? Who would I have been then?

Instead, we came to Australia, another generation of

colonists who called England 'home'. This time, the move became permanent: it became, not a temporary life defined by the work for empire, which finished, as for so many of my ancestors, with retirement to enjoy its rewards in the home country, but a redefinition. Gradually, it became clear that we would never go home.

And so the moorings that underpinned us shifted and loosened: the traditions that formed our families in England became rumours and myths, photographs and stories. As they retreated into symbols only, unreinforced by their material signs — houses, architectures, stones, landscapes, trees, flowers — they became both more and less powerful. We rearticulated what they meant, and the reality became frozen, a memory of what had been left behind in 1969 that was constantly reworked, a shabby cloth overdone with new embroideries, until none of us could see what was underneath.

We were the only members of our family on this side of the world. Our upbringing was strangely lonely: when we moved to Australia, we lived in the country on a small property, so we didn't have neighbours or casual out-of-school friends. The only thing that reinforced our us-ness was each other. Three means two and one, and our quarrels ran all ways: sometimes it was me and our youngest sister banded together, sometimes the two youngest against the bossy eldest, sometimes the two eldest against the spoiled youngest. But we were three all the same: I truly believed that, in the end, we were three. I believed it all the way to the end, when everything fell apart and we became one and one and one.

To be a Croggon or a Rowe became, in the family lore, a

question of core identity. The values assigned to these categories infected us and grew malignantly into choices we made
about our loves (I meant to write *lives*, but perhaps this mistake is felicitous). These labels, affixed to each of us directly
and indirectly throughout our childhoods, drew us into their
subtexts. The contested border between Croggon and Rowe
became a binary that persisted unseen beneath our later lives,
a flaw in the geography, like the shadow of an Iron Age fort
beneath a meadow.

Our youngest sister was unambiguously a Rowe, the most
like our mother. As for me, the eldest, I tended to waver over
the threshold, depending: sometimes I was also a Croggon.
My mother most often compared me to Granny Rowe, her
mother, or sometimes to her oldest brother, Tiny. Sometimes
she compared me to my father. It depended on whether I
was my father's good daughter or substitute mother, or his
bad son; or I might be my mother's good son, or a good or
bad daughter. My sister, on the other hand, was like Ma, my
father's mother. Marked unambiguously as a Croggon (how
strange that I use that surname and she does not), she was left
swinging between approval and disapproval: the only one of
us considered by Ma to be a 'real Croggon', a true daughter of
our father, which also made her an imposter daughter to our
mother.

I preferred to exist in neutral territory, if I could. Even
now, these invisible lines condition how each of us is placed
in the family: we are not simply perceived as ourselves, but as
genealogical symbols that in turn are inflected by the British
class system, romanticised and distorted through the murky

lens of exile. After I moved out of home, I tried to absent myself from these family demarcations.

(The relief when I left the country when I was forty, for the first time since I was sixteen. An irritation that was so constant I no longer noticed it simply vanished. I was just myself, adequate and inadequate, but without the constant chafing of who I was expected to be …)

The subtexts were the dangerous bits: I was 'artistic' *like a Rowe*, which meant *like a Rowe* I was bad with money. My sister was good with money *like a Croggon*, which meant *like a Croggon* she couldn't be a proper artist. As the marriage collapsed, to be *like a Croggon* was to be my mother's enemy, *like Ma*, the woman whom she hated and who hated her, and to be our father's ally.

After our father remarried, the system became even more complicated: who is the 'authentic' Croggon, the 'original' family or the new one? My mother, who bears the memories of a life in Cornwall, considers herself the 'original'. My father's answer was our erasure. There are no photographs of us in our father's house. Some of his friends didn't even know we existed: at a family gathering for my father's eightieth birthday, old family friends of my father were shocked to discover this shadow family, we three sisters, our children, that they had never heard of. That is another bitter truth, a whole sea of tears.

It's not hard to see how this damaged us, how this placed my sister apart. Before our mother left, our father was mostly absent, and so it was her categorisations that counted most, hers that were most articulated. Children, in any case, were our mother's work. Making a family, making a home, was her passion and her life; it was what she was trained to do from birth; and when her family splintered and broke, so did the purpose of her life.

She approached the business of making a home and raising us with an almost professional zeal, *Good Housekeeping* in one hand and Dr Spock's *The Common Sense Book of Baby and Child Care* in the other. Dr Spock, the giant among child-rearing gurus in the 1960s, was the first paediatrician to integrate psychoanalytic ideas into child care: he preached affection and flexibility, rather than rigid discipline. Earlier methods of child raising insisted on a regime of punishment, telling parents that anything more than a kiss on the forehead would soften and spoil their children, making them unprepared for the world. With the Vietnam War protests, he became controversial: conservatives blamed Dr Spock for the 1960s counterculture, children raised with the 'instant gratification' of their needs. I suspect we have many reasons to be grateful to Dr Spock, although he was inflected through older methods. Corporal punishment was part of our childhood; we were disciplined like horses and dogs.

Among other things, Dr Spock suggested that each child ought to be treated as an individual. My mother did this very consciously, but still we were ordered by categories that went beyond our individuality. My sister was the one who had her hair cut short, which she hated because people mistook her for a boy. My hair, on the other hand, was always shoulder length. It was our youngest sister who had the long hair, like our mother's in the photographs of her as a little girl. This was part of the natural order of things, and we ordered it according to the senses we made of it, conscious and unconscious. Her hair was short like Ma's. Our sister's hair was long, like Granny's. I was … in between.

It's hard to write this down, it seems so crude. And yet it's true: I know, we all knew, that this was how it worked.

We were only dimly aware, if we were aware at all, how these divisions expressed older histories, wider patterns. As teenagers, we felt so different from everyone else that it never occurred to us that we were typical, that our story was just one tiny detail in the gigantic system of relations that was the British Empire. Our whole lives were shaped by this machine, even though by the time we were born it was well in decline: our very biography, where we were born, where we lived, where we ended up, was determined by the global reach of British capital.

The first time I became aware of these larger patterns — stereotypes, if you will, a culture and an economy reproducing the lives of those who live within it into the same pattern — was when I read A.L. Rowse's autobiography, *A Cornish Childhood*. My father, the second youngest of four sons, was unable to inherit the family business, a leather-tanning company in a village called Grampound, midway between Truro and St Austell. He said once that he only had two choices, to become a farmer or a miner: and like his younger brother, who later became a mining executive and emigrated to the United States, he became a miner.

My parents married in 1961, and shortly afterwards my father got a job in Western Deep Levels, which still holds the record for being the deepest mine in the world, and he and my mother started their married life in South Africa. They lived in Carletonville, a small mining town not far from Johannesburg in Gauteng, a province of South Africa that holds the richest goldfields in the world. The town is named after Guy Carleton Jones, a director of Consolidated Gold Fields, and is still mostly privately owned by the mining companies. We were all born in the four years they lived in Carletonville, and so we have two birth certificates, South African and British.

It was the height of Apartheid. My mother had Black maids, who did housework. They would have lived behind the house, in servants' quarters, and were not allowed to have their families with them. I have no memories of them at all. My mother had a settler's paranoia about the 'natives', perhaps the result of earlier family lore about riots in India, which is why she owned dogs and refused to have a Black nanny. My father managed the 'natives', whom he called 'boys', who worked in the mine.

I stare at photographs of everyday life in Apartheid South Africa. The ones that fascinate me most are not the terrible photos of the riots, protests, and massacres, but those of the streets my parents would have walked through. Everywhere my parents went, everywhere we went as children, they would have obeyed the signs, entering buildings through the 'European only' entrances, passing butchers that advertised second-grade meat for 'servants and boys, 80c', sitting on park benches that were only for whites, or that were marked 'nannies only', visiting beaches that were signed 'WHITE AREA', 'BLANKE GEBEID'. They would have seen the protests on the news, the marches, the burning of passbooks. They've never spoken to me about these things, what it was like to walk through those streets. Perhaps it's a kind of shame. I don't know.

Whiteness isn't a colour. It's a sigil invisibly imprinted on those who possess it. As with the binaries of sex, we read its presence and absence into bodies and classify them accordingly. Whiteness shifts: its privilege may be given or withdrawn. In South Africa, my mother was almost reclassified as a 'coloured'. Her skin, she always said, tanned quickly, like her mother's, because of that Italian great-grandmother.

When we left South Africa, someone gave me a Black doll as a present, which I refused to play with. I know about this because it was retailed as a funny family story. I guess it was an amusingly 'natural' thing, a response that I, as a white child, could be said to hold instinctively. I think about it often, wondering what can be done about these formative conditionings, whether they are ever thoroughly expiated. But obviously, every single thing I encountered, every sign I saw (for I could already read), every encounter, everything I heard, told me that I was white and that I was superior to Blacks.

I learned to speak both Afrikaans and English. I remember nothing of the Afrikaans, a derivation of Dutch with a sprinkling of Khoisan, a group of African languages notable for using the click as a phoneme. It remains only as an echo of familiarity when I hear a South African accent, and perhaps in the fact that I find German syntax and diction transparent in a way that I don't find, for example, French. It often puzzles me, this lost language. Where is it?

Experts in child development say that the first three years are crucial in a child's development. I spent my first three years in the most racist country in a world that was deeply scarred and marked by racism.

Can I ever get rid of this? Is it so determinate that I can never escape it?

I have to believe that it's possible to get past it. Otherwise, there is no hope: not for me, not for anyone.

The whiteness

It was the whiteness of the whale that above all
things appalled me. But how can I hope to explain
myself here; and yet, in some dim, random way,
explain myself I must, else all these chapters might
be naught.

Moby-Dick

Not long ago, I went through all my early poems and looked
very hard at the word 'white'. What did I mean when I used
it? Did I mean: innocent? Did I mean: pure? Did I mean:
some subtext of race that I hadn't noticed until now? Did this
word exclude people who read the poem, in the same way that
almost all the poets I read as a child excluded me, because I
was a girl?

Sometimes I thought that it did. Where I couldn't be
sure, where it seemed too easy a locution, where it bore the

uncomfortable nimbus of unthinking, I looked for more accurate words.

There are always more accurate words.

In *Moby-Dick*, there's a whole chapter on 'The Whiteness of the Whale', in which Ishmael, Melville's narrator, attempts to describe the colour's peculiar qualities. He notes that white 'refiningly enhances beauty', and is associated with royalty, a pre-eminence that 'applies to the human race itself, giving the white man ideal mastership over every dusky tribe'. It's a virtue that he lists with many other appearances of whiteness through various cultures and times — associations of kings, empires, gladness, purity — as being 'sweet, and honourable, and sublime'.

When we look in the mirror, those of us with the mantle of whiteness, we perceive in our pallor Ishmael's magniloquent ascription of dominion. Ishmael lists its symbolic qualities through the histories of the patriarchs: the kings of Siam, the Austrian Empire, the white robes of twenty-four elders about the Throne of God. On the Hanoverian flag there is a white horse; behind the crown on the flag of the Austro-Hungarian empire is a white stripe. White, Ishmael tells us, is the colour of empire. With a deft sleight of hand, he implies that Rome possessed 'the same imperial hue'.

But the colour of Imperial Rome was purple, not white.

Textiles dyed with Tyrian purple were only worn by Roman officials, most particularly Roman emperors: the son of an emperor was described as porphyrogenitus, 'born to the purple'. The dye was extracted from several species of predatory snails, which secrete the purple mucus from the hypobranchial gland behind their anuses to sedate their prey. The snails were gathered along the Levant coast and boiled for days in lead vats, to extract the purple dye. The smell was famously disgusting, and clung to the textiles for some time after they were dyed. It took a quarter of a million snails to make one ounce of Tyrian purple, and so it was considered one of the great treasures of the ancient world.

According to Roman legend, the dye was discovered by Hercules, who was taking his dog for a walk along the beach one day when the dog bit a snail. When he saw that the dog's mouth was stained purple, Hercules founded the dyeing industry. But the Romans stole this story, along with the dye, from the Phoenicians, just as they stole Hercules from the Herakles of the Greeks. The Phoenicians said that purple was discovered by the pet dog of Tyros, who was the mistress of Tyre's patron god Melqart (or Melkarth or Melicarthus), who was also called Ba'al Ṣūr, the Lord of the City of Tyre. Melqart was the patron god of Tyre, associated with business, agriculture, and colonisation. Later, as Baal, he was named in the Bible as the enemy of God, and later still he is listed in the seventeenth-century grimoire *The Lesser Key of Solomon*, also known as *Clavicula Salomonis Regis*, as one of the Seven Princes of Hell, who can be summoned by the masters of the occult.

Back when he was simply lord of the Phoenician city of Tyre, he sauntered along the beach with his mistress Tyros and her dog, who picked up a snail in its mouth. When Tyros saw the dog's purple mouth, she asked for a dress of that colour: and that is how Tyrian purple began.

The first records of Tyrian purple turn up in Ugaritic and Hittite sources from the fourteenth century BCE. And now I read that one of the major sources of the dye, the red-mouthed snail, has vanished without trace from the Mediterranean beaches where it was once abundant, along with another thirty-eight species of the fifty-nine molluscs that once were documented on the eastern Mediterranean coast. In their place, the spectral white of bleached shells, just as Ishmael overwrites even the imperial purple of Rome with whiteness. 'Or is it, that as in essence whiteness is not so much a color as the visible absence of color; and at the same time the concrete of all colors; is it for these reasons that there is such a dumb blankness, full of meaning ... a colorless, all-color of atheism from which we shrink?'

Whiteness, the colour of erasure.

Ishmael, who may or may not have been Melville, for Melville was anatomising more or less consciously something that none of us could look at directly, because of the blinding dazzle of our innocence — let us say that Melville was beginning to say what many other people who did not bear the mantle of whiteness saw already in full bloody technicolour.

What he glimpses but can't quite articulate fills him with terror. 'There yet lurks,' says Ishmael, 'an elusive something in the innermost idea of this hue, which strikes more of panic to the soul than that redness which affrights in blood.' Or later: 'Is it that by its indefiniteness it shadows forth the heartless voids and immensities of the universe?' When applied to what is objectively monstrous — 'the white bear of the poles, and the white shark of the tropics' — this whiteness makes them 'the transcendent horrors they are'. In a footnote, he extrapolates: the 'intolerable hideousness' of the polar bear comes about because the 'irresponsible ferociousness of the creature stands invested in the fleece of celestial innocence and love; and hence, by bringing together two such opposite emotions in our minds, the Polar bear frightens us with so unnatural a contrast'.

So near, Ishmael. So near. He forgets that when we look in mirrors, we see ourselves backwards.

Ishmael's outrage is palpable: that monsters such as the polar bear and the great white shark, whose benighted monstrosity and hideousness should be properly expressed in blackness, should put on the white robes of 'innocence and love' is intolerable, even unnatural. They are 'brutes', words also used to describe human beings whom we wish to exile from humanity because of their animality (for human beings and animals exist in different orders of being: the lower humans, and especially women, closer to animals; the higher humans closer to God). Synonyms listed for 'brute' in the online dictionary: 'savage, beast, monster, animal, sadist, barbarian, devil, demon, fiend, ogre; thug, lout, boor, oaf, ruffian, yahoo, rowdy, bully boy; *informal* swine, bastard, pig'. It's not hard to read the racial fractures in these words, how easily they slip and pry open the borders of the human.

Moby-Dick was published in 1851. What a difference in a century and a half! Consider the 'irresponsible ferociousness' of the polar bear. They are now symbols of the wildness that is vanishing beyond reclamation, the bear who is drowning or starving to death as the northern polar ice caps melt and disappear. 'Polar bears,' says the World Wildlife Fund, 'are one of the most iconic and well-loved species in the world'. They are cuddly bears in Christmas hats and red scarves, playful mother bears with cubs on icebergs, duly domesticated to symbols of our generosity and mortality. Now the bear properly wears our celestial innocence.

Not so the great white shark, which still expresses that 'irresponsible ferociousness'. The shark resists the bear's domestication: it is too efficient a predator, too mysterious — too much like Ahab's monster, rising out of dark, unconscious depths with murderous intent. The hunt for the killer shark is a real thing, real enough that in 2014 the Western Australian premier Colin Barnett put aside $20 million to hunt down great white sharks, in an exercise that was both pointless and environmentally destructive. Perhaps Ishmael is correct: seeing in this animal an unbearable reflection of our own rapacity, we must erase it; its appropriation of our whiteness onto what we read as its irrational savagery is too dazzling. It's notable that those politicians who are most invested in the illogic of culling great whites also believe in the superiority of white Australia and the shimmering mirage of 'western civilisation'.

An average of six people a year are killed by sharks, but human beings kill 100 million sharks every year: so many that some shark populations are on the verge of collapse. The shark-fin trade is a major part of this, because the fins are a valuable commodity, selling for around $1,100 a kilogram.

The cruelty of this trade is immeasurable: when sharks are caught, their dorsal fins are cut off and their bodies thrown back, still living, into the sea, where they spiral down into the depths, unable to swim and therefore unable to breathe, dying of suffocation and blood loss.

There is an innocence that might properly belong to a predatory animal that over millions of years has shaped itself perfectly into its environment, as part of an interlocking set of interdependencies on which it and its prey depend, and which, through no fault in its own nature, is hunted to extinction or has its habitat destroyed.

Sometimes I think of Peter Ustinov, bon vivant, comic actor and writer, filmmaker, opera and theatre director, screenwriter, head of UNICEF, head of the World Federalist Movement, Oscar winner, tax evader, child of a more fortunate time of calamity. Whenever he had to write down his skin colour when entering the United States, he wrote 'pink'.

My skin is mainly a mottled beigey pale pink, coloured by the blood you can see through it. When I fell onto a piece of flint and cut a deep flap of skin off my knee, it wasn't white, more a sort of ivory yellow, the shade I will be, presumably, when I am dead and there is no blood to colour me in. When I was younger, my face was freckled; I have no freckles on my face now, but they are sprinkled over my arms and legs, growing darker with age.

Whiteness isn't really about skin colour. Like blackness, it's a category. I carry the mantle of whiteness into all my dealings, large and small, unconsciously, just as I carry the rags of class, my irredeemably bourgeois inheritance. I speak, write, think Englishness.

It's tempting to repudiate all these things, but that's too easy. How could I repudiate Blake, or Shakespeare, or even the King James Bible? It would be pointless, meaningless. Just as my ethics are shaped, whether I like it or not, by the Gospels of a religion that I rejected when I was seven years old, so my language has shaped the entirety of my writerly identity. They are part of what I am, for good and ill. I can begin from no platform of purity: like everyone else, I am stuck in the mess of history, where I was plonked when I was born.

There is a particular pinkness that belongs to very privileged middle-aged men: chief executive officers, senior politicians. You don't notice it when you see these men on television, only in real life: it's a sheen that reminds you of the petals of hothouse flowers, protected from the slightest bruising breeze. I met a couple of these men over some lunches in expensive restaurants that I was invited to when I was on an advisory panel for a literary magazine. I didn't do much advising, so I felt like a fraud, but I liked the treat of a meal that I couldn't otherwise afford.

There was always at least one of these men. They were famous men, their faces familiar from news reports and television shows. They all had a particular polish, an exfoliated smoothness. Perhaps I might have found this quality unremarkable on a famous woman, because women are supposed to devote care to their appearance, but it seemed qualitatively different. On these men, it was seamlessly part of the package:

127

the expensive fabrics of their designer suits, the shiny shoes, the confident voices. It didn't occur to me to think of it as feminine skin: it signalled itself as masculine, a sign of the luxuries that power affords. Well-hydrated, well-fed, well-monied, well-attended: the uber-pink of uber-whiteness.

When the Rachel Doležal scandal broke in 2015, I followed it, as many people did, with a kind of horrified fascination. It seemed like the extreme edge of something, a grotesque manifestation of white dysfunction.

Doležal 'identifies' as Black. She perms her hair into an afro and uses hair products that African American women use. There are photos of her in dreadlocks and weaves. She started sunbathing and used bronzing products to darken her skin. She became a prominent civil-rights activist, was elected Spokane branch president of the National Association for the Advancement of Colored People, taught Africana studies at university, was education director at the Human Rights Education Institute in Idaho. She is of German Czech heritage. As Black as I am. As white as I am.

'I felt this huge sense of homecoming with regards to the Black community,' she said in an interview with *The Guardian* in 2017. 'On the white side I noticed hatred, fear, and ignorance. And on the Black side I noticed fear, anger, and pain. I felt more at home with the anger and pain towards whites, because I had some anger and pain — toward not just my parents but also, even though I wouldn't have been able to articulate it then, towards white supremacy. I unapologetically stood on the Black side. I was standing with my convictions, standing also with my siblings, standing with justice.'

Photos show her as a teen: a blonde, freckled white kid. She recounts a horrific childhood (denied by her family) being raised in a fundamentalist Christian household. In 2002, she sued Howard University, a Black university, for racial discrimination against her, because she was white. The coloniser at work, ensuring she is entitled to every space, because no space must be unavailable for us.

She says in the same interview: 'There's no protected class for me. I'm this generic, ambiguous scapegoat for white people to call me a race traitor and take out their hostility on. And I'm a target for anger and pain about white people from the Black community. It's like I am the worst of all these worlds.'

The savagery of whiteness, its pettiness, its hypocrisy, its dishonesty, its murderousness: these are hard things to understand about oneself. I can understand why Doležal wanted to reject these things. Of course I can understand it. I want to reject them too.

'I am beginning to wonder,' says Ijeoma Oluo in her excruciating 2017 interview with Doležal in *The Stranger*, 'if it isn't blackness that Doležal doesn't understand, but whiteness.'

The pathology of whiteness is that it can't face itself. The merest glimpse of itself, in the monstrous savagery of the great white shark or the polar bear, generates the deepest repulsion. The self-pitying whiteness that believes, in its heart, that it is the true victim of those who argue against the injustice of whiteness. What is a 'victim'? Someone who has no agency, who is at the mercy of unjustly wielded power. According to the binary hinge that swings this way, that way, someone who is not at fault.

To victimise another person is an expression of power. So what could be more satisfyingly totalising than being able to victimise someone while *at the same time* claiming victimhood?

I watch the documentary, *The Rachel Divide*, with the same sick fascination that I followed the scandal. There's something specifically American about the story: the weird fundamentalist Christianity of her childhood, the obsession with moral purity, the quest to be a 'real self', the notion that persistence is a virtue in itself, no matter what is being willed.

I wonder if in writing this I am somehow doing the same thing Doležal does. It's difficult to conclusively say that I'm not. I am centring my own whiteness in the face of Black anguish. I am looking for some kind of redemption or, at the very least, a way of belonging in the world that has some kind of authenticity, even though I am forced to make it up myself. I am not in blackface, I am not that grotesque; but it feels uncomfortable to prod the traumas of my family, when there are so many others — Black people, people who were poor — who suffered to feed my family's privilege.

No doubt this is why white people need to identify blackness with suffering, as if it is nothing else but the mark of trauma. To recognise the reality of that suffering is certainly a wound to our self-respect, but our compassion restores it. We can turn from the crimes of our forefathers and become Good People. *But we are still loveable*, we tell ourselves. *We are still good. We must be.*

(I understand there is something inevitably grotesque about this self-examination. On the plus side, there isn't anything inauthentic about my particular heritage and history. I am absolutely, authentically, a product of my culture and language and class.)

I always refused the role of victim. This was often counter-productive: it made it difficult for me to see when I was a victim of things — sexual abuse or exploitation, for example. I would position myself in myself so I wasn't humiliated by my powerlessness: *I chose this*. Or more probably, *it doesn't matter*.

Refusals

I can't write this story in a straight line. Even as my fingers skitter across the keyboard, nimble and fleet from decades of flickering over thousands of words, millions of words, typing almost at the speed of thinking, I can feel myself, the me inside me, skewing my gaze so I am peering out of the corner of my eye.

Skewed. 'Suddenly changing direction or position.' Or more ominously: 'Make biased or distorted in a way that is regarded as inaccurate, unfair, or misleading.'

I want to be fair, accurate, honest. But some things can only be said skewed. Some things are skewed in their very being.

I have many of the flaws of the autodidact: a generalist imagination, undisciplined reading, partial knowledge. I've done a lot of catching up over the years, uneasily aware of my limitations — sometimes with laser focus, more often without.

I had, in any case, the first necessities to learn the things I wanted to learn: boundless curiosity, the ability to read.

I was once told by an academic that not learning the disciplines of academic writing permitted me a freedom in my structures of thought that he envied. That may or may not be the case; I learned the things I learned, in the ways that I learned them, and they have mostly served my purposes. Luckily, I didn't want to be a quantum physicist. I wanted to be a poet.

All the same, I find myself tempted to write something like a thesis, an account that takes on all the shapes of authority, that travels the authorised paths towards an impeccably argued conclusion. But something inside me rebels. Each shape of thought has its own shape. I can only speak in fragments, because always, always, since I first became conscious, I have been in fragments. Part of that is the business of becoming a self in the first place, which is about creating an illusion of wholeness over a reality that is always partial and multiple, in the same way we think of our bodies as singular when in reality we are constituted of 37.2 trillion individual cells.

My primary experience of consciousness is the desolating shock of becoming aware that I am individual, separate from others. Singular. I was a child who cultivated solitude. Later, consciousness became multiple: a continuous process of understanding relationship, the decentred self that is a part of a community, a node in an ecology: daughter, mother, wife, friend, colleague. Part of an inheritance, a culture, a continuation of a tradition.

Sister.

I don't want to be *inaccurate, unfair, or misleading*, but if I am to be wholly honest, I don't know how I can avoid it, either. It isn't possible to tell all the truth: there is so much of it, everywhere.

In my mid-twenties, I made two decisions that changed my life irrevocably. Neither of them really felt like choices, but the fact remains that I could have chosen otherwise, and if I had, my life would have been totally different.

The first choice. I left my job at the Melbourne *Herald*, after finishing a four-year cadetship and then one year reporting industrial affairs, because I wanted to write poems. Back then, journalism was a secure career with an assured future. When I resigned, a senior journalist at *The Herald*, Bill Hitchings, was very angry with me. He lectured me at length in the Phoenix, the rathole pub in Flinders Street where Herald and Weekly Times journalists went after work, trying to get me to change my mind. How dare I, he asked me, give up the privilege I had been given, the chance to speak to hundreds of thousands of people, for something as trivial as poetry, which hardly anybody read? As a journalist, I had the chance to change things, to make things better, to make people notice. A poet would make no difference at all.

Bill was old school, from a working-class background: a kind of journalist that hardly exists anymore. I respected him, and he was always kind to me; he was a straight-up man who, unlike some of his colleagues, was never a creep. He began his working life as a fireman on the railways in Wales, before he moved to London and started working in Fleet Street. He worked for *The Herald* for thirty years, covering countless royal commissions, major stories like the collapse of the West Gate Bridge, the Ethiopian famine, the Springbok tour of New Zealand. When I was at *The Herald*, he was reporting the trials of Lindy Chamberlain, convinced from the beginning that he was witnessing a terrible miscarriage of justice.

I knew Bill wasn't wrong. I didn't even have the words to say why I was making this choice. To Bill, my leaving journalism was criminal self-indulgence. I was considered a 'good journo'. I was being considered to cover Canberra, the first step to potentially more glamorous positions, maybe even an overseas posting. Bill was furious that I was throwing away the prospects that were in front of me, the *privilege* that was offered me. He knew what that privilege meant; he had fought for it.

I now suspect that if I had stayed and continued in the career laid out for me, I would have plunged through the depression that was already the texture of my life into something much worse. I didn't have any way of articulating the necessity that existed inside me. In my years as a full-time journalist, if I wasn't out at one of those endless drunken parties, lying in the back of a taxi watching streetlights blurring through the darkness in my head as I went from one to another, I would come home from work and cry for no reason. I wrote almost no poetry. I was toxic with what I couldn't say, what I couldn't perceive. When I handed in my resignation letter, I felt as if a huge weight had been lifted from my body.

It's hard to think back on a time when I was led almost

completely by inarticulate but overwhelming impulse. It's hard to know whether I'm remembering correctly, if I'm being accurate, or if I'm simply overlaying later justifications. But I remember that feeling of lightness.

I didn't know what I meant by wanting to write poetry. I had no plans. People asked me what I was going to do, and I had no answer. I continued freelancing, which then made me quite a good living. I kept finding cheques that I had forgotten to bank: it was the one time in my life that I had more money than I needed. I broke up with my sweet long-term boyfriend, slept with too many men, took up with a handsome Greek boy who was so much the opposite of the reliable husband my father wanted me to marry that he was perfect.

I had nightmares about getting married, a ceremony that I couldn't get out of, a brick-veneer house surrounded by a chain-link fence with no gate, panic and suffocation.

I wrote some poems.

The second choice came a year later. When I accidentally fell pregnant to the handsome Greek man, I decided to have the baby.

I mostly don't remember the act of writing, but I remember one poem: 'This is the Stone', which was the title poem of my first book (after my first title, *Quickening*, was refused because of another collection that came out the same year). I wrote it after watching a documentary about Frida Kahlo. It was the first time I had heard of her. Her paintings hit me with the force of revelation.

> it's when you want to shrug it all off:
> the gross pap of warm anaesthetised brain
> hotels ringing with stale tongues
> the bland translations of headlines
> walls everywhere
>
> when money's sensual brutality
> chats warmly in your veins
> when your possessions assert their tyranny
> mocking you from corners
>
> where is the moon's still wash
> over uncluttered landscapes?
> where are your lovers' mouths
> which stopped your mouth so neatly?
> in this dreamless city you put them away
>
> now you turn to a window
> which mimics you in ice
> your face a marble of loss
> your hair a curtain of dust:
> this is the stone you work on

I had never written anything directly autobiographical before; almost all my poems were fictions, personas, masks, displacements. To write directly of myself seemed like the greatest self-indulgence; there was nothing interesting in me to write about. But Kahlo used herself as her subject matter, pitilessly, magnificently. I thought that maybe I could do the same thing, and it mightn't be bad art: it could be blazing, magnificent, truthful. It was the first time I sensed that there might be a tradition in which I might not be a misfit, wrong-sexed: a tradition that permitted *me*.

When I wrote this poem, I was sitting on the floor late at night in my rented apartment with my new couch and my fashionable clothes and my bad housekeeping. I felt purely exhilarated, as if finally I was touching the edges of something that I had been looking for my whole life.

I didn't include this poem in my *New and Selected*: I think it struck me as too portentous. But it mattered then as a psychic placing of myself where I was, lost among the rags of my bourgeois self, unhappy, *dreamless*, *stopped*, *anaesthetised*. A statement of intent. A beginning.

Within a year, I was pregnant.

Totally off the rails, said my father.

Sometimes I have a nagging regret about my lack of tertiary education. There was a moment, during the six months I spent as a writer in residence at the University of Cambridge, a colonial oddity at high table — a woman smoking cigars and drinking port in the dons' parlour, deliberately ignoring the subtle English signs of exclusion — when I realised that

I could have been an academic. It was a glimpse of a possible parallel life, a path that had always been open to me, but which somehow I had never quite seen.

When I left school, the last thing I wanted to do was to go to university. Because I was good at exams (I have always responded well to stress), career counsellors suggested that I should study law. I revolted violently against it, not least because it was my father's dearest wish. I had also had enough of my peers: school represented years of misery, a low-level mist of constant anxiety that I remember only in patches. There are four years in particular, when my parents' marriage was disintegrating, that are almost completely blank.

School was humiliating, the usual story of being bullied and excluded. I was paralysingly shy, serious, bespectacled, so plain that I destroyed my school photographs because to look at them filled me with overwhelming shame and embarrassment.

I never learned to fight back. I had no idea how to. I learned to endure, to ignore the humiliation that comes with being the mark of bullies. I learned that girls were cruel, much crueller than boys. Even the goon who sexually assaulted me in class, deliberately shoving his finger into my cunt as I walked past and sniggering at his friends as he sniffed his hand, didn't hurt me as much as the girls did. I just pretended that he wasn't there.

I couldn't pretend the girls weren't there. They tangled me in a hierarchy that I was always failing to clamber up because I didn't understand its codes.

Through various accidents of bureaucracy, I was too

ALISON CROGGON

young to go to university when I finished school: I had skipped
two grades in primary school, so when I completed my HSC,
I had only just turned fifteen. I was academically capable, but
in every other way it was a disaster: two years in teenager
time is an enormous gulf. When I saw girls crying at speech
night, I was baffled: I couldn't understand how anyone could
be anything but relieved to be leaving school. For many years
afterwards, I would count the years out of high school — one
year out, two years out — as a continual arc of improvement.
Nothing that happened afterwards, it seemed to me then, was
as bad as what happened there.

My father's solution to the dilemma of what to do with
me next was to send me off on my own for eight months to
visit my relatives in England. I heard later that I was sent
with instructions: I was to be 'straightened out'. I was already
crooked, already skewing in undesirable directions.

It seems laughable, looking back. I was such a mild rebel: I
smoked cigarettes, my one persistent vice, and in my final year
of school I went to a few parties where I had kissed a couple
of boys. Desire was moving fiercely inside me, but I hadn't
worked out the mechanics. In my final year of school, I started
hanging out with my friend Anna. We smoked together on
long-distance runs, and on a couple of occasions went out
drinking to pick up boys. Somehow, we didn't run into trouble: even the boys who drove me home in their panel van on
the long, dark country road, when I had drunk so many Black
Russians that they had to stop at regular intervals to allow me
to throw up, didn't push it anywhere ugly. All that came later,
when I didn't care.

Those eight months in England were hard on the relatives responsible for the straightening, but they were much harder on me. My father washed his hands of responsibility for me, emotionally and financially, relying on others to pick up the problem. These relatives hadn't seen me since I was ten years old, when we travelled to England for a couple of months after the death of my paternal grandfather. They were being asked to take responsibility for a stranger — moreover, a stranger who was a fucked-up adolescent girl.

Money was sent at intervals, but I can't remember the details, and in any case it wasn't very much. I got jobs: at various stages, I worked in a caravan park, a hairdresser's, and a pub as a barmaid (I lied about my age). I had few social skills, and was very badly instructed; it didn't even occur to me that I should offer to pay board until my aunt told me, in a conversation I still remember with burning embarrassment as it dawned on me what a burden I was being to other people, as I realised why I was being shuffled from relative to relative, a nuisance that nobody wanted.

If I had been older, I might have spent some of those eight months having adventures in Europe, learning the pleasures of travel, doing the gap-year thing that became standard later, but I was too young and, I suppose, too afraid. I had no sense of agency, no conviction that I could arrange my own life. I passively let things happen to me, unable to conceive that I could make decisions about my life that had any real purchase. I set my jaw and pretended that I was fine, that I was totally aware and in charge of whatever was going on. I got so good at it, I fooled myself. I doubt I fooled many other people. It wasn't until my own children were fifteen that I realised how young I was then.

It wasn't all bad, but nevertheless, it left a scar. I didn't travel overseas again until I was forty years old, when I went to Cambridge and considered the academic career that, in a different life, I might have had.

My father, newly remarried, perhaps hoping that he could create a new life, untainted by his wayward daughters and ex-wife, washed his hands of all of us. For the final two years of high school, my sister changed schools, moved to Melbourne, and came to live with me, in my cheap, shabby flat in Prahran. She was barely sixteen. By then I was seventeen, working as a copygirl on *The Herald*, where I earned around ten dollars below the poverty line.

It seems like another age: I took home my pay in the yellow envelope for which everyone queued every Thursday outside the Herald and Weekly Times pay office. We typed stories on copy paper, which as a copygirl I 'ran' — literally carried the copy paper, one paragraph on each sheet of paper — from the journalist to the subs' room, where I put it in the copytaster's wooden box. The copytaster was called Alan Bain, a short, choleric man with encyclopaedic knowledge (he once gave me a lecture on the ranks in the Australian Army when I got a caption wrong) who did the initial fact-checking of the copy before it was sent to whoever was laying out the page. It was then sent upstairs through the vacuum tubes to the hot-metal typesetters, and then down to the second floor to be printed on the huge presses that shook the whole building at edition time.

It wasn't that long ago, but remembering it feels like peering into some kind of prehistory. The old Herald building was turned into fancy apartments with a fancy restaurant called the Press Club on the ground floor that was owned by George Calombaris.

My memory of this time, the years from when I was eighteen to my early twenties, is full of gaps. I can't quite place things.

I was the only person with a job, but I was earning poverty wages. My sister must have had some kind of allowance, but I can't remember. Again, when I look back with my own children in mind, it seems unbelievable.

Later, when I was still a cadet, we moved into a house with our youngest sister. In those days, a share house was always with each other: whatever conflicts there were between us were never as strong as the urge to stay together. We had no one except each other, no cousins, aunts, uncles, or grandparents to spread the load of our family identity. At the same time, we were tense with the fissions that hadn't quite exploded, the traumas and depressions that were then unperceived by any of us but which were already beginning to mark the courses of our adult lives.

A few years later, when I had left journalism to become a poet, when I was the newly sole parent of a two-year-old and a new baby, our youngest sister first became ill. She came to live with me in a house by the sea. There was no allowance: she had left school, so she was responsible for herself. That was when my father washed his hands of her.

I don't know why I assumed that it was possible to be responsible for my youngest sister as well as my children. I guess it wasn't a decision as such, but a situation that accumulated. The initial idea was that I would cover expenses in exchange for child care until she was able to get a job. She needed somewhere to live, and I needed someone to babysit when I was out reviewing plays (I had just begun to work for *The Bulletin*, a national weekly news magazine, as their Melbourne theatre critic). But rapidly it became clear that child care wasn't an option, and also that I didn't make enough money to pay the living expenses for four people. It should have been obvious from the beginning, but there was no one to tell me so, and anyway, it was what we had always done, since we left home.

I was blamed for how badly things turned out: our poverty, her eventual psychotic breakdown, my eviction when the police turned up when I was in bed with a stomach virus and gave me twenty-four hours to move. It was further evidence that I was *off the rails*.

My poor mother, frantically trying to help my youngest sister. On the same day that I was hurriedly packing my possessions and then sitting on a suitcase outside my locked house with my two small kids, waiting for a taxi to take me to the home of a friend, my youngest sister was psychotic and homeless on the streets of St Kilda, having been turned away from hospital.

I will always remember the kindness of the Chilean removalists who saw the Pablo Neruda among my books, asked if

I was a writer, and then quoted his poetry to me. When we were too late for the storage depot, because packing took too long, they kept all my things in their garage for free until I found another house. The kindness of my neighbour, who was also, as I remember, having a terrible time. I think about her sometimes, about how self-absorbed I was, how I felt she was judging me. It was only later that I realised her generosity.

I failed both of my sisters, although in retrospect, it's hard to see how I could have done anything else. As a fifteen-year-old fuck-up in Europe, or a twenty-seven-year-old fuck-up in Melbourne, I found myself in situations in which I could do nothing but fail. I have struggled to compensate for that inadequacy all my adult life.

I once thought that my father didn't love us, but nothing is that simple. He has at least acknowledged that he failed us, and in his own way, he makes amends. I remember how he fostered my passion for reading. I remember the peace of early mornings back home, when I would get out of bed at 5.30 am to be with my father, reading and drinking tea. I was jealous of those hours, and resented it bitterly if anyone else disturbed them.

My father was sent to boarding school when he was four years old. When I remember that, the first step of British imperial brutalisation, what he did to us becomes less inexplicable.

I worry that my father's actions are more explicable to me than what has happened between me and my sister. That's how the patriarchy stamps us: it funnels the compassion of women away from each other.

We share a whole history. It should be easier to understand.

Rage

I have sometimes thought that empathy is the great lie of literature, the great lie and the great seduction. And yet I also know, to my core, that a capacity for empathy is real. It may lead us to places that are not merely extensions of the self we know, may lead us beyond our self-closing knowledge. In those places, we may become strange to ourselves and may at least see ourselves in some kind of perspective.

The danger of empathy is that the empathy we think we find for others might be in fact only for ourselves. We can be so brilliant at projecting ourselves into the page that, under the guise of our magnificent empathy, we need never understand another person: the self becomes the entire universe.

I wonder about this with every word I write.

But maybe, maybe, maybe ... maybe an honest accounting of oneself might be the beginning of understanding others. It is such a gamble: perhaps I will be so misled by the miasmas of my self that I will end up, finally, lost in the same delusion that drove me here. Maybe all these words will betray me: maybe all I am doing is preserving my own lack of understanding, my cherished sense of innocence and goodness.

My sister's accusations draw up all my own protestations of innocence. None of us wants to be a monster. I know that any protestations will make no difference at all, because whether these things are true or not isn't the point. They are meant to be unanswerable.

My sister is one of the few people capable of driving me to the point where I snap, overwhelmed by rage and frustration. And that very breakage proves all my brutality, just as my complete withdrawal proves my callousness, just as writing this proves my ruthlessness.

I remember one evening, after our mother left her unhappy marriage, when I was about fourteen. My father was then commuting between our small property in Durham Lead, half an hour's drive outside Ballarat, and his job in Melbourne. The property was called Garibaldi, named by the Italian goldminers who arrived a century before us. They had left a mullock heap behind the abandoned schoolhouse that was across the dirt road that ran alongside our house. We picked daffodils in the schoolhouse grounds in springtime and took home old books we found in the cupboards. Our twenty acres had the remains of buildings, an old cowshed, a brick chimney, a bluestone-lined cellar that we turned into a fish-pond. My mother had bought a two-bedroom weatherboard that cost all of $750; it had been cut in half, put on a truck, and transported to Garibaldi. Before the miners, the land was named by the Wathaurong people who lived there, but I can't find what that name was.

My father arrived home late every night, maybe about seven in the evening. As the eldest sister, I adopted the role of the substitute mother, or perhaps it was bestowed upon me, since I also stood in for my mother when my father went to formal dinners. I am always becoming a substitute mother; it's a role I still fall into — perhaps I hope I can do it properly this time, perhaps I hope I can restore what was broken.

Certainly, I wasn't very good at it: both my sisters resented my assumption of authority. We quarrelled all the time, having no higher authority to appeal to in our differences. When our father returned home, he was too tired, probably too depressed, to sort things out. He told us to deal with these things ourselves.

That night, my sister wanted to pick a fight. I decided I wouldn't rise to the bait. We were in the kitchen that our mother had made, a small, cosy room with a black and white Rayburn stove and wallpaper of red flowers. Around the pine table that keeps turning up in all my descriptions of kitchens were an old church pew (against the wall) and old-fashioned cottage chairs. At each end of the table were the biggest chairs, thrones for the matriarch and the patriarch. I was sitting in the matriarch's chair.

She was throwing everything at me, picking every scab, every insult. I sat there, holding in my temper, refusing to respond to any of her sallies. I. Would. Not. Give. Her. That.

Satisfaction. I suppose it was very irritating. Finally, after maybe a half-hour or so of provocation, she kicked me in the shin as hard as she could, so hard that there was a lump on the bone for years afterwards.

Every inhibition snapped: I still remember the white, obliterating fire that tore through my head. I picked up the pepper grinder, which was a solid wooden weapon about the length of my forearm. I wanted to vent all my strength, leaving no reserves. I wanted to use every single bit of my physical strength to smash her to a pulp.

She locked herself in the toilet, jamming her feet against the door so I couldn't break it down. I threw myself against the door, but it wouldn't give, so I beat it with the pepper grinder, leaving dents in the wood. I am certain that I would have tried to kill her, had I been able to reach her. I have to remain grateful that I couldn't, that the door held.

No, I am not innocent.

Four decades later, I feel such sympathy for the fourteen-year-old that I was then, the twelve-year-old that was my sister. We were abandoned in a storm that neither of us knew how to navigate. We were already dealing with traumas that we had no name for. It was the mid-seventies, and divorce was still a scandal: none of my peers at school had divorced parents. Nobody told the school what had happened. My behaviour that year — back then it was called Leaving, now Year 11 — was entirely mysterious to my teachers: I had been a top-level student all through high school, and suddenly I was failing everything.

At that point, I wanted to be a vet, so I had chosen maths and science subjects. In first term my marks were good, but in the second term they went through the floor. When the chemistry teacher, Mr Tunbridge, read out my score of zero in organic chemistry to mock me, I wasn't even embarrassed. I didn't care. I guessed all my answers in my final exams, walked out after half an hour, and was honestly surprised that I did as well as 27 per cent.

Nobody knew what had happened until one day I walked into a class, dumped my books, and walked out. Someone found me crying in the library. Mrs Hewlett, who wasn't a teacher I had thought of as particularly nice, took me into a small room and wormed it out of me. I think things improved slightly after that, although the truth is that I don't remember very well. I was lucky I didn't have to repeat a year, which would have been wholly humiliating; instead, I shifted all my subjects to humanities. I did fine in the HSC exams.

In the 1970s, people didn't think about the effects of marital conflict or divorce on children. 'Children are tough, dear,' my father said to me, when he wasn't telling me that life wasn't fair. But children aren't tough. None of us came through.

I don't remember much of our final fight. We were talking over the phone. I remember pleading, no, don't bring that up, it has nothing to do with me, and my sister persisting, insisting, because now there was a gap in my wall, this tiny gap that was my compassion, that meant she could push through her 'narrative', the 'narrative' she kept talking about that I knew was about my guilt, her innocence, until that white obliterating flame surged through me and I just started shouting. And as I started shouting, she said, as a shield: 'But I have PTSD.' I remember spitting out in return, viciously: 'We've all got PTSD, darling.'

Complex PTSD doesn't stem from a single traumatic event, the kind of thing commonly experienced by soldiers or victims of violent rape. It occurs after long-term trauma. It's commonly experienced by victims of domestic violence, for instance, or by people who were abandoned or neglected at crucial parts of their childhood or adolescence.

None of us was actively abused, but in different ways, we were all abandoned.

For four years, which I barely remember, my parents' marriage was a kind of hell. My father began to only come home for weekends, and when he was home, the fighting was constant. I crawled into the hallway to listen to the arguments, night after night, unable to sleep. (When the neighbours fight, when I hear the man next door yelling at his wife, it brings back that feeling of hypervigilant helplessness, the compulsion to creep close and listen in the darkness, the sense that some kind of survival, my survival, is at stake.) I could hear my mother shouting, but not my father, who spoke quietly. There was always a fear that my mother would kill my father. We all know, without quite knowing how we know because we didn't speak about it for years, that she stabbed him once. He was always gluing back together the pottery mugs that she threw at him.

Me, a frightened twelve-year-old, comforting my mother as she sobbed uncontrollably, as she climbed into our beds, screaming at my father not to touch her. And then, one day, when she was forty, she left. I felt a dazzling sense of relief that there would be no more fighting.

The physical violence I remember was all my mother's. She was the one who smacked us, she was the one who threw things across the kitchen when she lost her temper. But underneath that was a much more insidious kind of violence that was less visible.

My father was an executive, and drew an executive salary. My mother never knew how much my father earned, and she certainly never saw any of it. He gave my mother forty dollars a week — the equivalent in 2017 of $454.94, according to the Reserve Bank's inflation calculator — to cover all the household expenses. These were solely her business, 'women's business'. In 2018, the poverty line for a family with three children, excluding housing and education expenses that my mother didn't have to pay, is $864. My mother brought us up on a sum that was roughly half what is now considered poverty. It was why our school uniforms were full of holes — she couldn't afford to get our kilts dry-cleaned or to replace our school jumpers or to buy us new clothes. We never went on holidays, like other people.

Even the house was budget price, as my mother thriftily saved money. My mother sanded and painted and wallpapered the walls, with our help. She built all the yards outside herself. Because there wasn't enough money for food, she raised calves for meat and kept milch cows and hens. We had a chip heater for hot water, and a water tank, and a washing machine that ought to have been in a museum.

(The old Georgian farmhouse that my mother had lovingly renovated in Cornwall was sold when my father decided to stay in Australia, and none of us saw any of that money, either. When my father remarried later and built a new house for his new family, he was able to pay for it outright. He furnished it with the antiques my mother had found in chicken coops and junk shops in Cornwall in the seventies. Then she had bought them for a few shillings; now they're worth thousands.)

Having never worked in her life, my mother got a job as an advertising rep on the local free newspaper. And then she moved out. At first, she rented a flat, and then she bought her own house. She left us with our father because he told her he would fight her for everything, the children, the house. Maybe she was too tired to fight. She thought, she told me, that he would look after us, even if he didn't look after her, because, as she was fond of saying, we were 'his own flesh and blood'.

When we left home, my father expected us to support ourselves completely, which we did, mostly badly. When, thirty years later, my father gave me $2,500 after an unexpected windfall, I was astonished. He had never voluntarily given me any money in the whole of my adult life. (Even then, it didn't come from him, it came from his wife.) When I left the handsome Greek man, seven months pregnant and with a toddler, to live with my youngest sister, he offered to guarantee a loan from the bank for $5,000.

If he had had no money, I would have understood. I have never had much money, but I would never leave my own children to twist in the wind. But he did have it. He always did. We were middle-class kids with a middle-class education, but we were raised on a poverty income. Everything we owned, even our clothes, was second-hand. Even my private education cost nothing: I had two scholarships.

I kind of resent that. I wish I had cost something, something that said I was worth it.

These are all old, stale injustices. I have long forgiven them, although I can't forgive the structures that made them possible. But I see every day how they have trapped my mother, financially, emotionally, in their consequences, and that unfairness still stings. Even now, she lives frugally on a pension and carer's allowance, while my father gets by comfortably in the house he bought with capital that was accumulated through my mother's sweat.

Back then, it was so easy for us to blame our mother. In the dark interiors of my parents' marriage, she was the one who complained, the one who made the noise, the one who shouted. Outside the home, she was too proud to ask for help: it would have been humiliating, shameful, an admission of failure.

When people feel there isn't enough to go around, conflict can be vicious. Maybe that's part of what happened between me and my sister, that sense that there was so little of everything. There wasn't enough money, there wasn't enough love.

Everything turned into a deadly competition. And we both lost.

Prisms

Instead of being a common place from which we could build some kind of understanding, all this history ever did was force us apart. I guess that's what people call 'lateral violence'.

The contempt that flowed through me when my sister talked about PTSD, the contempt that always has filled me when women, in the midst of conflict, suddenly take refuge in their gendered fragility to prevent any comeback: *I am more hurt, more frightened, more weak, than you: to do anything but agree with me is monstrous.* When I read women of colour talking about 'white women's tears', I think of all the times I have seen white women do this (no woman of colour has ever done this to me, and yes, it is something that is *done* to another person). I think of a board meeting where another woman deflected some critical comment by bursting into tears. It disarmed all the men, who rushed to comfort her, glancing reproachfully at me, and any further discussion was at an end.

I would rather hide my vulnerability. I would rather fight on equal terms, to win my arguments on the basis of what is argued rather than emotional manipulativeness. (In this world, of course, there is no such thing as *equal terms*.) It's pride, a revulsion against the mortification of being seen as a victim. That meant that even when I did become a victim of something, I was unable to see it. It took me thirty years to understand that I had been raped, that I had been sexually victimised, that it wasn't my agency that caused these things, but the agency of other people who did me harm. I carried the harm without realising what it was. It was only when I saw other women speaking about their own experiences, when anger rose inside me at the injustice of what had happened to them, that I recognised that it had also happened to me.

That recognition was unexpectedly painful, unexpectedly humbling. It meant I had to understand my own lack of power.

I think of my mother telling me how nobody ever rushed to support her in all her difficulties, because she always tried to cope, to be a *good wife*, while the women who complained and wept were swamped with attention. That reluctance to ask for help, to sue for mercy. The idea that one must take it on the chin and get on with it.

Where did that come from? It's not so bad to ask for help. It's not so bad to have compassion for oneself. I have had too little pity for myself. My sister has nothing but pity for herself. Neither of these things is good.

My mother often told me that I was not *feminine* enough. I was raised steeped in an ideology that insisted on the femininity of women, and yet my mother, despite her insistence on our necessary femininity, was never quite feminine either. She built fences and sanded walls and pulled calves out of muddy dams and tamed horses. When I was grown up and started wondering where I got this idea that it was totally possible to both work and be a mother, it took me a long time — too long — to realise that I learned it from my mother. One thing I have never felt is the guilt other women have told me they suffered from working.

My mother passed on to us the codes of her own upbringing. She was raised to be a wife, a good wife, the wife who I see in the 1960s *Good Housekeeping* recipe book, relaxing in a cocktail dress to welcome her husband home from work after a day managing her children in her modern kitchen. She taught us the code of subordination to men: that one must never, for example, 'undermine a man's authority', one must always fly to attend and conceal from others a man's hurt, a man's weakness. The man, I was told (but not in so many words), is always vulnerable, but this must never be mentioned — it must always be covered up, disguised, compensated. This is part of the duty of being a woman.

I decided early that I didn't want to be *feminine*, to buy into this unholy code in which I could be nothing but secondary. Perhaps this pride is partly about that. I think also that part of the reflexive contempt that I feel when women expose their weakness as a defence is that they are pulling on the conditioning that insists that women must protect men from their own weakness.

Women know (white women know) — because they understand the power of patriarchy — that this weakness is a locus of power. *Male* power. When right-wing ideologues speak of 'strong women', they mean women who use their own strength to compensate for the weakness of men. When men rush to protect women who employ this same weakness, it seems to me that they are also rushing to protect themselves.

I don't despise people for revealing their vulnerability, because that is sharing something that is part of human experience, our common skin: it's an exchange of trust. But too often I see women, white women, weaponising their perceived weakness, turning it on those who express legitimate criticisms of their behaviour. I see powerful, wealthy women threatening to sue those who have criticised them — people poorer than they are, women of colour, or trans women — who are simply asking not to be hurt or marginalised. I see how quickly an aggressor can make herself a victim.

I think of my friend Ange years ago, back when we were both young single mothers, cynically observing kids fighting in a sandpit. 'The one who starts crying first,' she said, 'is usually the one who hit first.'

'Strategic tears' is a behaviour Ruby Hamad describes and analyses in her book *White Tears/Brown Scars*. 'White women,' she writes, 'are more powerful than ever but they cling to the role of the damsel in order to both exert and deny their power.' It's a kind of devil's pact, formalised through centuries of behavioural conditioning.

On one side, the overt weakness of women that must be

protected by men. On the other, the covert weakness of men that must be protected by women. And at the core, the lie of this weakness itself, which is not weakness but a kind of power that men and women silently vow to preserve together.

And what are we all preserving?

Aye, there's the rub.

Women of colour know what's being preserved. The people my people colonised know. When I read their accounts, I recognise too much. I measure what they say against what I know, all the minute details that amount to a life's experience, my own behaviours and thoughts. This cycle of brutalisation, of petty competition for power, it all matches, far too uncomfortably. When I reach the end of Hamad's book and discover that she sees discomforting parallels between the characteristics of narcissistic personality disorder and white supremacy, I gasp out loud.

Hamad lists the classic symptoms of NDP noted in the *Diagnostic and Statistical Manual of Mental Disorders* — 'grandiosity and self-importance; preoccupation with fantasies of unlimited power, brilliance, beauty, and success; self-belief in their own special and unique status that can only be understood by other similarly special people; a need for excessive admiration; a sense of entitlement; interpersonally exploitative behaviour; envy of others and/or the belief others envy them; arrogant and haughty behaviours; and a profound lack of empathy' — and says: 'Every single one of these applies to whiteness on a fundamental level. Every one.'

I also note that Hamad is sceptical, as I am, that narcissistic personality disorder exists as a mental illness of an individual. The manual does describe a recognisable cluster of behaviours, though, behaviours that are enacted through the shifting networks of power that constitute our social and economic relationships, and which very often, in our capitalist, white supremacist society, are rewarded.

I sometimes think that the most important book I ever read was Edward Said's *Orientalism*. That first reading: enthralled, horrified, more and more ashamed as I realised that the mirror he was holding up reflected my own face. It was the first time I consciously recognised how empire shaped my life. It wasn't only responsible for my abiding sense of dislocation, my feeling that I don't belong anywhere. It reached into the very DNA of my thinking.

This figure I see in the foreground, this me. How monstrous am I? What does it mean to be a monster? From Latin monstrum, meaning an abomination, an object of dread, a divine portent, to its usage in Middle English, 'strange and unnatural'. From the mid-fifteenth century: 'unnatural, deviating from the natural order, hideous'. Grotesque, hideous, ugly, ghastly, gruesome, horrible, horrid, horrific, horrendous, horrifying, grisly, disgusting, repulsive, repellent, revolting, nightmarish, dreadful, frightening, terrifying, fearsome, freakish, malformed, misshapen, unnatural, abnormal, mutant, miscreated.

I was born as part of a monstrous structure — the *grotesque, hideous, ugly, ghastly, gruesome, horrible* relations of power that constituted colonial Britain. A structure that shaped me, that shapes the very language that I speak and use and love. I am the daughter of an empire that declared itself the natural order of the world.

My paternal grandmother hissing at me in her kitchen in Cornwall, when I was fifteen: *You're not British.*

I quite honestly did not understand what she meant, although I felt the weight of her accusation. Of course I was British. What else could I be? I had spent the past decade being teased at school in rural Victoria for my English accent. It was on my passport. How could I be anything except British?

From my grandmother's point of view, I was the product of a marriage that had ended in a disgraceful divorce, staining the reputation of the Croggons. I was the daughter of a woman she had never liked, although notoriously, my grandmother, the mother of four sons, didn't like any women. But perhaps also … perhaps I had been too long in the colonies and was too deeply infected by strangeness and foreignness. I permed my hair and smoked cigarettes in Truro cafes while reading women's magazines, which was seen by villagers and reported to my grandmother as a scandal. I said I was an atheist, which seemed of no great moment to me, but shocked my grandmother deeply. I was a girl, a young girl, although I didn't think I was young at the time — I was so young! — blindly budding into her sexuality.

I was already beyond the pale.

Beyond the pale means outside the boundaries. It comes from the Latin, palus, which means a fence stake.

The Pale was the name given to a strip of land across Ireland that, in the late Middle Ages, marked the parts of Ireland under English rule. The laws that governed the Pale were laid out in one of the Statutes of Kilkenny: 'A Statute of the Fortieth Year of King Edward III., enacted in a parliament held in Kilkenny, A.D. 1367, before Lionel Duke of Clarence, Lord Lieutenant of Ireland.'

Whereas at the conquest of the land of Ireland, and for a long time after, the English of the said land used the English language, mode of riding and apparel, and were governed and ruled, both they and their subjects called Betaghes, according to the English law, in which time God and holy Church, and their franchises according to their condition were maintained and themselves lived in due subjection; but now many English of the said land, forsaking the English language, manners, mode of riding, laws and usages, live and govern themselves according to the manners, fashion, and language of the Irish enemies; and also have made divers marriages and alliances between themselves and the Irish enemies aforesaid; whereby the said land, and the liege people thereof, the English language, the allegiance due to our lord the king, and the English laws there, are put in subjection and decayed, and the Irish enemies exalted and raised up, contrary to reason ...

'Contrary to reason', which is the reason of the Divine Right of the King. Reason said that the English were forbidden to marry the Irish, or foster Irish children, or sell them horses, on pain of excommunication, confiscation of their property, and death as traitors. They were forbidden to use the Irish language or Irish laws, which were 'bad customs' and not laws at all. They were not allowed to ride without saddles or play Irish sports like hurling or quoits, and they had to learn archery or lances because then they could fight properly against the Irish.

Hearteningly, because Edward didn't have the resources to ensure that everyone who played quoits went to prison, everyone ignored the laws and married whom they liked and dressed how they liked, and by Tudor times everyone in Ireland was speaking Irish.

It's fascinating that these laws don't force English language or culture upon the Irish: their first concern was to control their agents, the English settlers, who had to remain English in order to further the authority of the Crown.

The first concern of empire is that those who are responsible for its administration are properly stamped in the empire's image. But obviously in fourteenth-century Ireland, the culture of the conquered exerted a strangely powerful attraction, absorbing the settlers into it, transforming them into enemies of the Crown.

Eventually, the English state worked out that it wasn't enough to control its agents: it also had to stamp out or subjugate the cultures of those whom they colonised. Not only because those peoples could then be used to reproduce the empire themselves, but also to prevent the servants of empire 'going native'. The shame of miscegenation.

When my grandmother told me that I wasn't British, that's what she meant. I was already infected by the culture of the place in which I was supposed to represent the Crown of England. I was already a traitor.

Fault

Is it suitable to speak of fault? Is this small catastrophe that is our non-relationship my fault? Is looking for fault the right question? It seems to me that assigning fault between us simply reproduces the same tired patterns of recrimination, a fog of claims and counterclaims that darkens the air so we don't have to see the truth.

She and I, we did okay, all things considered. Our youngest sister suffered the worst, but this isn't her story, and I have no right to speculate what happened to her. Nor is it my sister's story, except in how it intersects with mine. I don't know her story at all: I can only glimpse it through the distorted lenses of our dysfunctional relationship. All I know is what she's told me, this story in which I merely fulfil a role in which I, as a feeling, complex person, am absent. (I know her pain is real; this only makes everything more complicated, more difficult to perceive.)

The nearest I can work it out: I represent my necessary guilt, which creates her necessary innocence.

I am looking for the template that makes this pattern.

How possible is it to know another person? I understand that we can never really know even our intimates, but she has brought me to the hard kernel of that hard truth. How possible is it to really know ourselves?

I remember walking along a street in Northcote, my children, very small, walking beside me. I had been shopping, or was going shopping. I crossed the street, calling the children to my hands, and quite suddenly a memory erupted into my consciousness. I felt vertigo, a sense of falling, a horror so intense I halted in my tracks. Almost as soon as I thought it, the memory vanished completely, leaving not even the slightest clue of its context. Its only shape was the trace it left behind, my memory of that sensation of ice flooding through my body.

I still have no idea what it was. I can only remember the completion of its erasure, as if my brain, in that moment of shock, decided to annihilate it. I have never found a way back.

Scrabbling in the midst of this rubble, wondering what the hell happened, turning over these inadequate proofs, these unreliable data.

I have evidence, which is often misleading, but which nevertheless may corroborate a narrative. (My narrative.) I have letters, emails, objects, photographs, cards. I have kept them all, over all these decades. I have witnesses, with all their attendant inscrutabilities and contradictions. I have the traces in myself, the habits and behaviours of a self shaped over a lifetime. I have the least reliable thing of all, my own memory.

I have these words, which simultaneously expose and conceal, which undo truth and undo lies, creating more truths, more lies. And here I am, doing what I do, building yet another narrative in the midst of this howling absence, making yet another beginning.

Least tangibly, but most importantly, there is love: the love that moves inside me, the love that others show me. This has always seemed to me an inexplicable and miraculous thing. How is it that something like love exists in a world that I have always known to be cruel and irrational? But love shines, real and tangible, right here. Despite everything. In the middle of everything.

I used to assume I loved my sister, despite everything, in the middle of everything. I used to think it was something that was simply there, the love of kin, a bedrock loyalty that existed beneath all of the superficial conflicts; I thought this love was something that could be assumed, that it would be there in the final accounting. There was always that teasing will-o'-the-wisp dancing before me: *this time* we will finally sort it out. *This time* we will properly understand each other.

Perhaps the most painful thing is that I don't believe that anymore. What I thought was my love for her was an emotion that doesn't exist, because the person I assumed she was doesn't exist. I have been as prone to fantasy as she was. Perhaps she felt some love for me at some point, but if so, it has all been eaten away, corroding into a smouldering hatred for the monster she says I am. (Or is that true? It's only part of the truth.)

I can only trace this process through her accusations. She has said on so many occasions that I wanted to destroy her. It always dismayed me that she thought so. Sometimes it made me angry. Sometimes I tried to show her how this wasn't true, using the methods that would work with me: reason, searching through the darknesses of childhood for the unspoken forces that shape and distort our behaviours, working through contradiction towards something like reality. For her, this method was aggression: her story became simpler and simpler, more and more damning, the more I attempted to open up our complexities.

For many years, I worked towards this infinitely deferred future, a future in which we might at last understand each other, but any peace we made always depended on my concessions, my silences, my forbearance and compassion. It's been a long time since I have confessed any intimacies to her, because anything I did say was used in evidence against me. I mostly wasn't conscious of that retreat: it just happened slowly, year by year, until I realised that I was telling her nothing.

Then there was that final attempt to get her to listen, to *hear* me, to *see* me: but the only thing it revealed was what she really thinks I am. (Not *who* I am; she doesn't think I'm a person. Yes, this reflection is bitter.)

How can any of this be love?

Eventually, I realised that she said that I wanted to destroy her because, in fact, she always wanted to destroy me.

I am the eldest, there before her, blocking out the light. I was never anything but in the way.

Unravelling

I've made several attempts at autobiography: countless poems, a novella. All of them are obsessed with beginnings. Part of me seems to think: if only I could pick up the right thread and wind it in, I could find my way through the labyrinth to the centre. Maybe I could find and slay the monster that laid the curse. As if there is a single thread or a single monster or even a single labyrinth. As if words really can find truth.

First memories. I am in a cot somewhere in South Africa, watching my parents back slowly towards a white wall. On the wall is a kitsch mass-produced picture of a generic African scene, a sunset maybe with a palm tree, in brightly contrasting colours. There were two of them, I remember, but those pictures didn't come home with us to England. As my parents back away, I am overcome by the terrible dread of nightmare. I didn't understand this memory until I had my own babies, and realised that my parents were trying to put me to sleep.

I suspect this was before anyone else was born, and if so, that means I was younger than two years old.

There's another vague memory, which might be from earlier than that, another time that I was in a cot: a glimpse of white gauze draped over me, perhaps some kind of mosquito net. But this is little more than an image. I have almost no direct memories of my sisters, or indeed of anyone else, from that period. I was the first child; I had two years being the focus of my mother's attention.

I remember, and this is still a South African memory, trying to remember what it was like inside my mother, which must have happened after a conversation with my mother about the baby inside her. I didn't understand why I couldn't remember anything before I was born; coming up against that blankness was maybe my first encounter with the puzzle of my own consciousness. How was it that I was there — which must be true, because my mother told me so — and yet I could remember nothing at all? It was as if I existed and didn't exist at the same time. Even then, I thought memory was a thread that bound me together into a single self. And even then I found myself holding a broken string, staring into the darkness.

How many times have I picked up that string, hoping this time that I will find my way through the labyrinth? The definition of insanity, they say, is doing the same thing over and over again, hoping for different results.

And here I am, again. Getting my eyes tested aged eight, this time in Australia, because somebody has finally noticed that I can't read blackboards. The chair that is so like a dentist's chair, a clumsy, heavy frame over my face, as the optometrist clicks through different glass lenses. I'm squinting, trying to see all these letters in focus, probably anxious not to fail this test, as I have always been anxious, although failing an eye test is a nonsense.

Which lens is clearer? This one? That one? This one again? This one?

Click. Click. Click.

My memories of childhood have clear divisions. I was born in Carletonville and lived there until I was four years old. Between the ages of four and seven, I lived in Cornwall, England. We left England on the SS Orcades when I was six. My father flew over by plane, which was the luxury option at the time, leaving my mother to travel alone with three small children. We landed on the day before my seventh birthday, a day fixed in my memory by crushing disappointment. On the ship, if you had a birthday, your table was decorated with streamers, and the stewards served you a birthday cake. I was looking forward to this celebration with all the greed of a child who only had sweet things on special occasions. When the ship docked a day early, I missed out.

After we arrived in Australia, we lived for a couple of months in an apartment in Royal Park, Melbourne. We could walk across the park to the zoo. And then we moved to Ballarat, in the Western District of Victoria, where I lived until I left home at fifteen.

I have always known that some of my memories are false. There's one, a South African memory, in which I am lying down in a darkened room. I can hear someone walking up my ear canal. Thump thump thump, like footsteps down a corridor. Finally, I sit up, and a tiny witch on a broomstick flies out of my ear.

I am not in the least surprised. I knew she was in there.

I know now that what I heard was my pulse, my heart pumping blood through my head, but the adult gloss doesn't remove that vivid image. My tiny witch circled around my head and disappeared. I don't remember being afraid — if anything, I was delighted.

Another memory from around the same time: my first sight of the stars. As a well-disciplined child, I was sent to bed with the witches well before dark. Being up late was special. In this memory, I am, I think, held in my father's arms, staring up at the sky, and it's a carnival of miraculous orbs — crimson, emerald, sapphire, gold — blazing in the darkness. I still remember the disappointed fall of my heart when, a few years later in England, I next saw the night sky. The modest freckling of tiny white stars bore no resemblance to the flamboyance I remembered.

That tiny witch isn't a dream. It carries exactly the same quality of conscious experience as my memories of being on the ship that took me to England when I was four, looking down from the ship into Durban Harbour at a sea full of red jellyfish. It was no surprise to me that some scientists now believe that memory is deeply related to imagination. Maybe fiction writers know this instinctively.

I'm pretty sure I'm not alone in the default assumption that my memory is a type of constantly rolling news footage, an impeccable ongoing record of my life. Maybe we need this assumption to get through the day. But consciously I know memory doesn't work like this at all, that the neurological workings that create memory are a constant dynamic process of storage, shuffling, and retrieval that occurs not in the past, but in the present. We remake our memories every day, every time we recall them. I am remaking mine now.

Even now, after decades of research, neurologists don't fully understand how memory works, but they do know that our memories are continually revised. They exist as neural pathways in the hippocampus, and are strengthened with use, which means that the more we remember something, the more we remember it. Sometimes we do remember things that didn't happen. And events can be erased.

Thinking about memory is like stepping into a hall of mirrors, in which anything like truth constantly retreats. How can we know the reality of anything, if even our personal memories might not be real? Memory is the primary way we build the narratives we know as our selves. Consciously and unconsciously, we craft our memories to support our vision of who we are, creating coherent subjectivities that we tell ourselves are rational, reasonable, and truthful.

But we can't know anything for sure. Both our personal and communal memories consist of a series of constantly negotiated agreements about the nature of reality. And quite often, as a quick saunter through the wilds of internet conspiracy theories (or even the history of science) will confirm, we are entirely capable of being profoundly mistaken. The human capacity for delusion isn't so much a bug as a feature. It's probably the basis of all our pretences towards civilisation.

Sometimes people straight-out lie, creating an alternative reality to conceal a truth they don't wish to be publicly known. But equally, we can be deceived, sincerely believing realities that don't exist. We can believe that our inevitably partial knowledge is the whole of reality. We can suppress things we consciously know in order to preserve a cherished perception, until that perception is, to us, the only true reality. There are so many ways of not seeing.

And yet, despite everything, I still believe in the human capacity for truth. Or at least, I believe in the possibility of striving towards truthfulness in good faith, a critical oscillation that uses the gifts we have, as conscious human beings, to evaluate what we know and what we think we know against the available evidence — which maybe is the closest we can get to truth. But we can only do this if we sacrifice the comforts of certainty, even about ourselves. We have to own up to being unreliable narrators.

There's always that tiny witch.

I've lost about a decade, between fourteen and twenty-four. I can remember isolated incidents, as if I am zooming into close-up, but when I try to recall it as a period of time, it's as if those ten years are covered in mist. I fell pregnant when I was twenty-five, and after that everything snaps back into focus and becomes a legible chronology.

I suspect that the real sources of my sister's grievances are lost in this mist, that the unhappy, lost, depressed, imperfectly recollected person that I was at that time committed all sorts of heinous, careless, and hurtful acts. I can remember some actions that make me flinch — things I did to other people, not to my sister. The fact that I can't remember absolves me of nothing, but neither does it absolve her. We were both fuck-ups of the first order.

It took me a long time to learn how to trust women, because, for me, to be betrayed by women is a much deeper wound than to be betrayed by men. (Maybe that was because the betrayal of men is woven into our expectations, betrayal and forgiveness; but women, we can't be forgiven.) My mother, at least consciously, never betrayed me: she has always been loyal to us, sometimes embarrassingly so. In all the quakes of my life, she was there.

I did betray her.

When I read Freud on mothers and daughters, I laughed out loud. Why is it, he asks obtusely, that daughter reject their mothers? It must be an innate catastrophe that happens around twelve, when the girl realises that her mother doesn't have a penis. The Oedipal drama means that she is forced to face her femaleness as lack (of a penis) and herself as castrated. I thought of myself as a little girl; if anything, I thought of the penis as an absurd extra, a ridiculous embellishment. I never wanted a penis. I never thought of myself as lack.

Since then, so many women — Clara Thompson, who

in 1947 proposed the idea of 'social envy', or Hélène Cixous, who insisted that women write out of their various bodies — have argued with Freud. What I realised as a little girl growing up was that my mother was a second-class citizen. And if my mother, as a good patriarchal woman, reinforced that secondary status by training her daughters in its conventions, conventions that permit boys authorities and freedoms and privileges that are denied to girls, the little girl resisted. In a patriarchal family, a little girl has two choices: to submit to the laws as laid down by her mother, who is subject to her father, or to be a bad girl. She can betray her mother or betray herself. Her mother, in a patriarchal family, has no choice. She enforces the rules. If she doesn't, she's a 'bad mother'. And no mother wants to be a 'bad mother'.

Betrayal was written into the contract when we were born.

My sister accuses me of hiding 'the truth'. I have no interest in hiding 'the truth'.

I know she betrayed my trust on countless occasions. I also betrayed her. There was, for example, the time I told her to put her finger in the mouth of a pair of pliers, and then closed them. When she started howling, our mother rushed in and told her off, because she was the one making the noise, and then our mother hit her with the pliers. I have zero memory of this, but I fully believe it happened.

Events like these are the normal rough and tumble of being siblings. In unbroken relationships, they become part of the family idiolect, the jokes I see my own children sharing with each other. This passing of juvenile wounds into hurtlessness never seemed to happen between us. One of the things that remains obscure to me is why we could never negotiate past those childish conflicts. I still don't understand how our relationship evolved into this toxic, impossibly tangled adulthood.

Back to the paradox. How do I apologise for sins I never committed? Is that, perhaps, the point? That if she accuses me of things that I know, beyond even the vagaries of memory, that I never did, and which I therefore will never apologise for, she can at last be rid of me?

Today, a colleague, an archivist, texts me a photo of a writers-festival program that she collated twenty years ago, which included a reading of a play of mine. At first, I have no idea what the play is, no memory at all. *Ananke*. What the hell was that? Gradually it filters back: it was a monologue about sexual abuse and imprisonment, written in full-on Shakespearean pastiche, adapted from my first long prose work, which switched between fiction and autobiographical essay — the first time I tried my hand at this sort of thing.

There was a time when my sister and I made things together. We collaborated (or at least, I thought we did). We made things happen. We co-wrote a radio play once; nothing came of it, but I remember the seriousness with which we worked, scribbling on foolscap in our tip of an apartment. Yet all my memories have been shuffled and rearranged, and I no longer trust them: what I thought was the case, what I assumed, is now under suspicion. I look back on the evidence of those times, on photos when we are laughing together, with astonishment, as fantastic relics from a time I am not sure even existed.

I'm trying to remember where I lived in those years, between 1979, when I moved to the city from the country, and 1985, when I resigned from *The Herald* to become a poet. It's a bit of a struggle. I can't quite place things.

At first, we lived in that flat in Prahran, forty-five dollars a week rent, and then another. All of us were very poor: I had my ill-paying job; my sister was a high-school student and then a tertiary student working part-time. After she left school, there was no further financial support from our father. There were other people living with us at various times: a housemate who was an old friend, my first boyfriend, and also, at different times, waifs and strays who had nowhere else to go, such as two high-school girls who ran away from home.

Then, for a couple of years, there was the house by the railway line in Prahran that we shared with our younger sister. After that, I lived by myself in a flat in St Kilda. I know that was in 1984, because it was the year I was an industrial-relations journalist. After I left *The Herald*, before I became pregnant, I moved into a smart one-bedroom apartment, again in Prahran. That was the only time in my life when I had spare money, when I could buy whatever clothes I liked and have a facial every month. I bought an expensive couch, covered in a tasteful floral fabric that was mostly white and which deteriorated rapidly once I had a baby.

That was probably the time in my life when I most despised myself, when an emptiness at the centre of my being began to become perceptible to me. But even then, consciousness only exists in patches. It is hard to think about these years, not because it's painful, but because I can't discern any continuity. So much seems to be missing.

It's like I was half alive.

One isolated memory, from when I was living in St Kilda. I'm sitting on a tram, eating an entire packet of biscuits, maybe smoking cigarettes (you could smoke on public transport in those days), deeply absorbed in some magazine — maybe *Cleo*, maybe *Cosmopolitan*. I was throwing my rubbish on the floor, completely oblivious, until a young man, who had been watching me with disgust, told me off. That was a moment when my perspective shifted, when a shell of self-absorption broke open and I saw myself through someone else's eyes. I was the very image of oblivious, self-centred, middle-class privilege.

That inability to see myself was a protective device. It was how I got through the humiliations of school. One time, I was appointed to deliver an opening prayer to the assembled school. I learned it by heart, but once I was standing in front of hundreds of people, I completely forgot every word. Coming off stage, shaking, people said to me, 'You poor thing.' I shrugged them off: it didn't matter, *it didn't happen*. Another image out of the mist: a ring of girls around me, mocking the kilt I was wearing, part of our winter uniform, because it was dirty, because it was too small for me, because all the edges of the pleats were threadbare and beginning to fall apart.

Our uniforms were always worn to death, I suppose because my mother couldn't afford to replace them often enough out of her housekeeping money. For the same reason, we had highly mockable school lunches made out of crumbly homemade bread, because she kept within her budget by making all our bread. (How we longed for that soft, aerated white bread …) We had two jersey cows we milked every morning and evening, and we raised poddy calves for meat. This was the preserve of my mother, the image of thrift and productivity, making a life out of what was given her.

I didn't want to see myself, because what I saw was too humiliating. I armoured myself in obliviousness. As a child, I hid in books: it was a family joke that when I was reading, almost nothing would rouse me. That same conscious obliviousness enabled me for many years to be a poet in a culture in which poetry is not valued. It gave me a space in which I could invent a self that wasn't possible otherwise. And perhaps my sister cultivated a similar obliviousness, for similar reasons.

We can't afford it anymore: not her, not me, not those wounded by our numb oblivion. We erased ourselves because we couldn't bear ourselves, and in doing so, we erased all the others.

Part of what I didn't want to see was that I was a woman, a vexed thing to be in a society in which women are still a category considered not-quite-fully-human. The odd thing is that, for all that, I liked being female. As a young woman, sexual desire was quite straightforward for me. I was voraciously heterosexual: I desired men as a woman desiring men. For some reason, I wasn't ashamed of it, in the same way that, although as a plumpish young woman I had the usual body-image problems, it never bothered me enough to actually diet.

What I felt within myself wasn't ever something I was ashamed of, although what I saw of me was a constant source of embarrassment and humiliation. When I look at old photos, I feel sorry for that young woman. I had no reason to think I was ugly, but I believed, to the core of my being, that I was. I liked sex, because in sex I was never ugly. In the realm of touch, I was beautiful.

Some aspects of feminine conditioning didn't quite take with me. When I was born, the first grandchild on both sides of the family, I was a disappointment to my father's family, because I was a girl. He went on to have two more girls and no sons, which became part of the failure of his first marriage. My mother, like my father, had only brothers. Neither of them really knew what to do with daughters. I suspect that as a young child I was partly, subconsciously, raised as if I were a boy.

I used to think it was something like what sometimes happens in a flock of chickens if there is no rooster: one of the chickens starts behaving like a rooster; it stops laying and starts to crow. (Friends of ours had a chicken that actually did change sex, growing a wattle, rooster feathers, and other secondary sexual characteristics, but that's a rarer thing: they're called gynandromorphs and are twice sexed. They supposedly occur when an egg is fertilised by two sperm. Inevitably, the chicken was called Henry.)

Being a substitute son gave me some imaginative space. Certainly as a child I was a tomboy, although I don't remember anyone calling me that, and I never thought of myself as particularly a boy. I don't think I thought of myself as particularly a girl either. I didn't play with dolls: they bored me. I loathed it when my mother insisted on forcing me into party dresses for visits to other people's houses. I remember, at about seven, staring at myself in a full-length mirror, despising the frilled red dress I was wearing, angry that I had lost my battle to wear something else. I longed for jeans and a windcheater, which I didn't have, because we couldn't afford them.

One of my favourite games was building huts for myself. Some of them were quite sophisticated: I even started to build one with a wooden frame, using bark for the roof like the early settlers and paving it with a brick floor. I never finished it, but its frame stood beside the dam for years. I spent hours with a boy I knew, part of the family who became our substitute cousins, building landscapes of earth and turning on the hose so we were gods of water, directing the rivers through an intricate web of courses and dams.

Writing, I assumed, had nothing to do with whether or not I was a girl. Even before we came to Australia, writing was a central part of my identity. The story is that I made my parents teach me my letters: I can remember tracing dot-to-dot alphabets my father drew for me. I know I could read before I went to school, because on the first day of school, a teacher drew an 'e' on the blackboard, both the proper way and backwards, and I knew the 'e' was backwards. Reportedly, I wrote a poem that day. Certainly, long after we moved to Australia, my primary school teacher Mrs Wilton wrote me letters in which she said that she looked forward to one day buying my books. Many years later, when I had begun to understand that my gender did have something to do with my writing, I sent Mrs Wilton an ill-chosen bunch of poems that included a Whitmanesque rant about cunts, which shocked and disappointed her. I had turned into the wrong sort of writer.

However I negotiated my gender as a prepubescent child — the truest thing I can say now is that I actually don't know — the world of writing was boundless. Almost as long ago as I can remember, I was going to be a writer. I was going to make worlds, and in those worlds, I was in charge. I could be whatever sex I wanted, and I could imagine anything I liked, and it had nothing to do with what kind of body I had.

I sustained that illusion for a long time. It lasted into my early twenties, until I first began to encounter the world of literature, which is different from the world of books that I lived in during my childhood. The first time I became aware of gender was listening to someone talk about writing as a woman at a Poets Union event in Melbourne when I was about eighteen. She talked about how difficult she found it to imagine a male character, how men couldn't imagine female characters. I listened in astonishment: it had never occurred to me that I couldn't imagine a male character because I was a woman. I thought that was what writers did, they imagined themselves as other people.

Male writers told me on several occasions that I wrote 'like a man', as if it were a compliment. Even then, I found that a surprising and uncomfortable comment; even then I knew I didn't want to 'write like a man'. I didn't want to *be* a man, because obviously I wasn't: I just didn't want to be secondary to men. 'That's me, the writer, him,' says Ursula K. Le Guin in her wonderful essay, 'Introducing Myself'. 'I am a man. Not maybe a first-rate man. I'm perfectly willing to admit that I may be in fact a kind of second-rate or imitation man, a Pretend-A-Him.'

I resented more than I can say that men stole the world of writing for themselves, and said it was wholly their province, solely an attribute of masculinity. I knew that it was my birthright, as much my right as anyone else's — and I didn't see why I had to sacrifice my sex in order to take it.

Before I had children, it wasn't surprising that I rejected the *feminine*. It wasn't a conscious decision, which made it merely reactive and therefore damaging. Like a female conservative politician, I placed myself as an 'exceptional' woman, transcending the limitations of her sex.

I refused to cook for boyfriends, not ever. If they wanted to eat in my house, they had to cook for themselves. I seldom had anything to do with preparing food at all after I left home; I only started to cook regularly after I had babies and had to, because otherwise we would all have starved.

This meant that when my sister and I lived together, all those decades ago, when we were in our early twenties and I was learning how to be a journalist, she did most of the cooking and shopping and household duties. And I think now that I would have treated her as the *feminine* that I rejected. I think that here she has genuine cause for complaint: she has said that I was not respectful of the work she did, that I was careless and ungrateful. For that I owe her an apology. I am ashamed that I treated her this way.

I have no memories of doing this, but I don't have any trouble believing that I did act this way. It's more likely than not that I fell into the patterns of behaviour that I already knew. They were the only patterns I had.

Our families, if we have them, know us from the very beginning. They have all the inside knowledge about who we are, the privileged views of intimate histories. What is the fantasy of being an orphan, the staple of so many children's stories, except the chance to decide something about the self that hasn't been decided by the family?

Yet what families reflect back can be more like funhouse mirrors, where aspects of the self are returned to us distorted and awry, grotesquely exaggerated or diminished. When I look at my adult children, their faces are underlaid with memories of their other faces, all the way back to babyhood. Every now and then, there is a little quake, which reminds me that my children exist far beyond what I know of them, that my perception of who they are is filtered through a template that is out of date. I'm chatting with my son, and suddenly, for no reason I can trace, I'm thinking, who is this man who is standing in my kitchen? Part of me thinks he is still ten years old; part of me settles lazily on an old perception.

Is it that simple? Is this chasm between my sister and me

simply about her loading up the present with the unaddressed and unexpiated crimes of the past? (But of course it is. There are so many pasts.)

Money

Sometimes when I think of the inherited, accumulated wealth that somehow has never trickled down to me, I feel a little aggrieved. If I had, for example, been given the deposit for a house, as my father was given for his first family home, I would not have to rent, with all the insecurity that comes with that.

But there's also a sense of relief that there are some privileges that I don't need to account for. The only things I own are fiscally worthless: books, computers, furniture, countless objects like my daughter's artworks or a tiny brass duck left to me by my grandmother, rugs we bought when we were flush, copyrights in my own work.

Maybe my neurotic attitude to money has been, in part, a kind of penance. It's also ignorance (why was I never taught not to be afraid of accounts at school?) and fear (that feeling, every time I signed a document in a bank, that I was forging my own signature). Part of it was certainly a rejection of the protestant parsimony of my father.

My father carried fiscal prudence to an extreme — all our childhood we suffered from it. Casual days at school were routinely humiliating. I particularly remember a pair of flared dark-brown hipster trousers with orange tartan cuffs, which my mother probably thought were cool, but which I knew, from the burning embarrassment I suffered when ironic compliments were directed my way, were too bright, too ugly. They made me stand out, when I only wanted to blend in. My mother did the washing for a family of five with her ancient machine: it was an open, round tub with a manual mangle at the top, to squeeze the water out of the clothes. She was constantly asking for a newer machine, but we never got one until she left and my father had to do the washing himself. Ha! Ha! How we laughed. (We did laugh, but it was bitter laughter.)

If that was fiscal prudence, I wanted nothing to do with it, in the same way that I wanted nothing to do with being feminine. But neither of these were conscious decisions: they were just reactions.

I had long guessed how our childhood played into my attitudes to money. But after my sister and I stopped talking, I also realised that somewhere in the rifts of my subconscious, I believed that being good with money was her territory. Not mine. *She* was the sister who was 'good with money'. *I* was the sister who was bad at it. We both believed this. This division came with all sorts of contradictory heft in the fucked moral universe of our family. Money, as Freud and Marx both knew well, represents so much more than an abstract value of exchange. It's loaded with values, almost all of them harmful.

I've joked all my life about my complete incapacity with money. Nothing has made me more anxious than dealing with finances. Trying to do my accounts caused a fog in my brain, a feeling near panic. I sensed, with the same primitive instincts that locate danger, that money is something that invalidates me, that cancels me out. I was afraid of it, afraid of its mysterious mechanisms. I loathed it, and yet it ruled my life.

I now realise that I can work out my finances like other people do; that even with my unstable writer's income, I can exercise some agency and decision. All I had to do was to learn some skills. Ignorance can be remedied.

It feels a little late in life to reach this understanding. In fact, it's mortifying: I look back on the chances I have had, at how I didn't even recognise that they were chances. In the same way I look at photos from my twenties and thirties and feel sadness for that young woman who always believed she was plain, I look back at my advantage and wonder how I squandered it. I wonder why I never quite believed in myself. My sister didn't believe in herself, either, and for the same reasons I didn't. And I see now that neither of us had the tools to repair the things that were wrong, not for ourselves, not for each other. Our mutual dysfunction was profound. And through our adult lives, the patterns set up between us in our childhood didn't dissolve: instead, they were insidiously reinforced.

A few decades of poverty did nothing to help me believe that I could be any good with money. I thought it was built-in, like my nose.

Before I was in my fifties, I had no idea, until an accountant added it up, how much I earned in a year, I couldn't read my financial records, and I didn't possess the smallest notion of what to do if I did. To me, all these things were as punitive and arbitrary as the love of God, which passeth all understanding.

Even now, writing this down is giving me a strange feeling of anxiety: I'm tight chested, as if I have asthma. I stand up, leave the desk, clean the house. The vacuumed carpets feel smooth and pleasing. The bathroom in this shabby rental will never look like the sparkling, hygienic bathrooms in ads; it's a refugee from the seventies, with a floor made of tiny tiles that one by one are breaking and lifting, and you can see a thin line of daylight through the cracked wall in the toilet. But it smells clean, like earned virtue.

I guess, as much as these territorial borders were inherited — and they were — they also mapped out our needs for differentiation. When we were little, our mother called us her *three little piggies*: there are photographs where we're all dressed in identical dresses, red with white sleeves that I think were marked with strawberries or cherries. I think I can even remember our mother making those dresses, sitting at her sewing machine, the fabric whirring over the table, in the Georgian farmhouse in St Austell that my mother renovated with such hope, imagining she would stay there, that we would bring our children there to visit her when she was old.

So long ago it seems like a different era. I remember

forests that are now towns, a time when rain puddles were full of tadpoles, a world that was not yet on the brink of vanishing completely. So strange, to see my life dwindling into history.

We all have animal instincts about territory, but how we express them, how we live them, is conditioned by the specifics of who we are. I am very territorial in a house: there is a chair that's my chair, and if someone is sitting in it when I want to, it makes me feel uncomfortable (if it's a family member, I throw them out; if it's a guest, I'll politely sit somewhere else). I watch the cats fighting off the white and ginger tom who lives down the road with terrifying screams and yowls, and I have a fellow feeling: I will chase him off too, this is our territory, mine and the cats', not his, and he isn't allowed here.

The possession of land, its commodification, is a European thing. Nigerian feminist Oyèrónkẹ́ Oyěwùmí describes how, in Yoruba culture, land was traditionally held by families, and given as gift: it wasn't until the English came that it became possible to buy and sell it as a commodity. For Indigenous Australians, land is country, a belonging invested with self and story and ancestry, a system of relationships that stretches far beyond western understandings of ownership. As colonists, settlers in a landscape in which our own long history is absent, we have a reductive idea of what land means, although I think many of us have a shadowy feeling that it means much more than territory, much more than a sum of money, much more than a fact of ownership.

I remember how so many farmers in the Western District hated trees. It always puzzled me: there were places with whole groves of ringbarked eucalypts, stark white, dangerous, pointlessly murdered. How our next-door neighbour cut down a locust tree, the only shade in one of his paddocks, but left the stump, so he still had to plough around it. Ownership of land in Australia so often meant a kind of hatred.

For most of my life, I coped with my fear of money by not coping with it at all. I didn't know how much I earned, only that it wasn't enough. I told myself that being bad with money was just part of being an artist. (The problem with my logic there was that, while it's true that being poor is part of being an artist, being a fiscal basket case, as I was, doesn't have to be.) It was easier to be a romantic anti-materialist back in the 1980s: money went further in those days. Money didn't matter to me, except when I didn't have it. I had no agency at all in relation to money, and I thought that meant that money had no agency over me.

I was a poet: how could money possibly matter to me?

Poverty has long cured me of any romanticism about starving artists, but even so, rags of that attitude hobbled me for almost all my adult life. Poverty has a moral weight: my lack of career and financial stability was, on one side of the family dichotomy, a sin, and on the other side, a sign of an admirable aristocratic disdain for material things. (An aristocratic disdain for material things is only feasible if you have material things.)

All my life as a writer, right up to my few moments of 'success', my father told me to 'face reality'. What he meant by that was that I should get married and 'settle down'. I didn't want to settle down: that seemed to me to be a kind of death. The thought of marriage literally gave me nightmares.

Nevertheless, I tried. In my early twenties I had a steady job and a steady boyfriend and I grew steadily more and more depressed (I can see it now, although I didn't then). Everywhere, my life was mapped out before me. I would continue as a journalist, rising through the ranks; I was already being groomed to be a national political reporter, and maybe then there might be an overseas posting, and then whatever. People who were my peers then are now running media empires. And my kind and gentle boyfriend would, at some unspecified time, ask me to marry him, and then we would move into the house that he had already sensibly bought as an investment property. And perhaps, further away than I could possibly imagine, there would be children. I would probably continue writing my poems, as the hobby that they presently were — not the central, defining work of my life, but occasional verses, which perhaps would one day be published in a slim, privately printed book.

I threw that life away with terrible violence. My father was furious, because I no longer had a man to take care of me (this was what a man was for, to take care of me). I didn't want to be taken care of, not one bit, but I was in no state to take care of myself either. I was the last person to cope with an unstable income.

As a cadet journalist, I didn't need a bank account, because I used the Herald and Weekly Times Credit Union, which was upstairs, and didn't really seem like a bank. As a full-time employee, I barely had to manage my money at all: it arrived every fortnight with the tax already deducted, and then I just paid for the things I had to pay for. I threw away the umbrella of full-time employment at the worst possible time, when I had children. My income plummeted and I had no skills to manage it.

There were a few years of terrible poverty in my late twenties and early thirties, first as a sole parent, and then living with my partner, who was also a writer and possibly worse with money than I was. When I was a single mother, I didn't pay my rent for an entire year: my landlady was astonishingly forbearing, and waited until I could pay her (which I did). There were times, too many, when the house was full of red, unopened bills, when every week was about the problem of getting through the next week. Looking back, I honestly don't know how we survived those times: they exist in my memory as a constant succession of humiliating negotiations. We got through by never squarely looking at the disaster, but that only extended it.

It was different, all the same, from the poverty that many poor people experience. It wasn't generational poverty, for a start (although I feel a pain in my heart when I hear my children talking about the deprivations of their childhoods). Even in the worst moments, there was always a possibility that a door might open, and being poor then wasn't nearly as hard as it is now.

I couldn't go on social security, because my income was far too ridiculously unstable to even contemplate negotiating the forms of what was then the Commonwealth Employment Service, now mostly replaced by Centrelink. (Years later, when robodebt became a thing, I felt an immense relief that that choice hadn't been open to us.) Even with a partner, finances were roller-coaster, feast or famine. One of us would win a prize or a commission or a grant, and suddenly we seemed to be rich: there were treats for everyone. Then there'd be no other income for the next six or twelve months. But we were always hopeful. There would be another stroke of luck. Something would happen. And something always did.

For about four years, something really happened: my fantasy books became bestsellers, mainly in the United States. For a while there, I was earning the salary of the average manager via royalties (although it didn't work out so well if I factored in that the books took me ten years to write). That was when I ran into real trouble, because I still had all the bad habits of poverty: I still didn't think past the next week. I certainly didn't think about the next year. I assumed that the money would keep on coming in, that I was a success now.

It didn't keep coming. In the past decade, author salaries, even those of popular authors, have dropped precipitously. I ended up with a nightmare tax debt that I couldn't possibly pay. It kept me awake at night, staring into the darkness, wondering why, as someone who was capable in so many ways, as someone who could solve all sorts of problems, I was so incompetent. Finally, on the advice of my accountant, a gentle man who was used to dealing with artists and who had a legendary bedside manner, I went bankrupt to clear the debt. Adding up the value of my property was a salutary experience: as I ticked 'no' down all the boxes that asked for the value of my house, of my yacht, of jewellery, of shareholdings, investment properties, I finally understood that, in the eyes of the world, my life was worth literally nothing.

After that, I began, painfully, to learn. It was sticky, there was still a fog in my head, part panic, part incapacity. But then, after I stopped speaking to my sister, there was suddenly agency. *Yes, I can do this.* I still feel as if I am driving through a dark forest in a car with no headlights (a feeling I don't actually know, as I can't drive). But I'm getting older. I don't have thirty years of prudence behind me. I have no safety net.

Everything I do is too late.

Inventing man and woman

Henrik Ibsen reportedly kept a scorpion on his desk. Every now and then, it began to look sickly: when that happened, he would give it a plum, which it would attack with its stinger, injecting it with its venom. And then the scorpion would look not so sick.

I experienced writing poems like that: it seemed to me that the desire to write poetry was a kind of internal poison that would build up over time until it became an intolerable pressure that had to be expressed — extracted, forced out, expelled. That would bring a sense of relief, until the poison began to build up again.

I thought of the poetry as a sickness, although the sickness wasn't the poetry itself, but whatever it was that made me want to write. Enfolded within my desire to write poems was a desire never to write them again. Sometimes I thought that I would be writing poetry until I wrote the poem that meant I could stop.

When I discovered I had a self, writing became a technology for creating me. There were other, more mundane, reasons attached to the compulsion to write. When I was a miserable schoolgirl, writing fuelled my fantasies of a future life, in which I became famous, important, respected: a Writer. I would return as a Famous Author and all the people who so despised me would be forced to apologise for treating me so badly.

As I grew, so too did my doubts and suspicions about the tools with which I did the building. There's good reason for this: these tools have been given to me by canonical writing, much of which I still love. But even as it opened up freedoms and possibilities, it enchained me. Mostly it wasn't written for me, a woman trying to think about her life in the late twentieth century. It was written for the men of letters, the cultivated man. *Homo literatus.*

In this drama, I was at best the passive vessel in which a man's legacy might be gestated.

When we think, we make categories in order to make things thinkable. This is obviously useful, because everyone does it. In the west, we sort reality into orders and hierarchies, from the lowest angels to the highest, tracing our systems back to Aristotle.

The problem with sorting into categories is that it's too easy to perceive only difference. The only aspects of reality that are considered significant are the edges of things, rivalries, kingdoms, territories. The notion of interrelationship — between people, between ourselves and other living creatures, ourselves and our environments — becomes a sentimental superstition. We begin to forget permeabilities, likenesses, kinship, which are put aside as naive, or signs of weakness. The fantasies of abstraction, money, and power become the only *real* realities, and these delusions lead us into madness. We dig up ancient swamp forests and burn them, as if the explosive release over two centuries of sixty million years of patiently stored sunlight will have no effect on our delicately balanced atmosphere, as if the ash of our delusions won't suffocate everything we know and love.

All living things are categorised, in order to make the dazzling, teeming variousness of life comprehensible. Scientific taxonomies run from the general to the particular: human beings, for example, are in the domain of Eukaryota, the kingdom of Animalia, the phylum of Chordata, the class of Mammalia, the order of Primates, the family of Hominidae, the genus of *Homo*, species *Homo sapiens*.

These classifications were sketched out by the Swedish botanist Carl Linnaeus in 1735, in his magisterial *Systema Naturae*. Just as alchemy is the forgotten sister to Newton's physical observations, European fantasies about race went hand in hand with Linnaeus' taxonomy. 'If flowers could be sorted by colour and shape,' says Angela Saini in her sweeping survey of scientific racism, *Superior*, 'then perhaps we too could fall into groups.'

In the tenth edition of *Systema Naturae*, published in 1758, he laid out the categories we still use today. He listed four main flavours of human, respectively corresponding to the

Americas, Europe, Asia, and Africa, and each easy to spot by their colours: red, white, yellow, and black. Categorising humans became a never-ending business. Every gentleman scholar (and they were almost exclusively men) drew up his own dividing lines, some going with as few as a couple of races, other with dozens or more ... Linnaeus himself included two separate sub-categories within his *Systema Naturae* for monster-like and feral humans. However the lines were drawn, once defined, these 'races' rapidly became slotted into hierarchies based on the politics of the time, character conflated with appearance, political circumstances becoming biological fact ... And so it began.

Linnaeus' taxonomy was later extended by Johann Friedrich Blumenbach, who is considered to be the father of anthropology. His refinements of Linnaeus' taxonomies persist to this day: Caucasians, from Europe, the Middle East, and North Africa; Mongolians, from East Asia; Ethiopians, from sub-Saharan Africa; Americans, the native peoples of the New World; and Malays, the peoples of Oceania. As Saini observes, he elevated Caucasians — his own race — to the 'most beautiful of them all'.

Those ideas are still current, monsters swimming in the depths of scientific discourse that, more and more frequently, rise into the light and show their teeth. It's not hard to see Linnaeus in the dubious 'race science' that's making a popular recurrence. There are so many examples: a book called *A Troublesome Inheritance* by Nicholas Wade, former science reporter for *The New York Times*, restates unfounded shibboleths about the essential genetic differences between races. There's Nobel Prize winner James Watson, co-discoverer of the DNA helix, who has insisted on many occasions that Black people are genetically inferior to white people, or the political scientist Charles Murray and sociologist Richard Herrnstein, a behaviouralist, who co-authored *The Bell Curve*, in which they argue for eugenic social policies that discourage poor or Black people from having babies.

From taxonomies we derive hierarchies, the higher and the lower. The binaries of sex are a fault line running through all these taxonomies. Women are lower than men, but where categories cross, the hierarchies become more complex: a Caucasian woman ranks higher than an Ethiopian man. It's only 'natural'.

The higher we place an animal or an angel, the more we conceive of it as being able to suffer pain. Friedrich Nietzsche thought that the higher a man's intellect, the more perfect his capacity for anguish: the ability to suffer was the mark of his superior humanity, the sign of the Übermensch. Everywhere in Christianity is the notion of suffering: physical suffering as a code for the higher spiritual suffering. The man nailed onto a cross, dying in agony as the sun darkens. And it's understandable, since it's impossible to conceive of a life without pain, that as a species we seek some kind of reason for it. It's understandable, perhaps, that since pain is inevitable, some people glorify it, turning it into a virtue, a spiritual sign.

In the worlds that Nietzsche lived in and responded to, the world of nineteenth-century men (a world that, for all our shiny technology, we still inhabit), suffering only existed if it could be articulated. Those who couldn't satisfactorily articulate their suffering — babies, children, women, animals, disabled people, the colonised — were not deemed to be properly conscious: they suffer too, but without awareness. It's not really considered to be suffering; it's not numinous with the romance of human consciousness. If it makes itself heard, it is only as complaint.

Back in the day, I barely registered the misogynies in the canonical works: I simply, almost without noticing, negotiated around them. Like most women, most 'others', I had been imagining myself into and around these narratives since I first started reading. I wanted to be a hero — but the proper stories, the significant events, the important adventures, always happened to men. These misogynies and their proliferating cousins were part of the ground structure of intellectual existence: in many cases, they were the qualifiers of intellectual seriousness.

I began to hate categories. I used them all the time, and I still use them, because they are useful, but I began to treat them with deep suspicion.

Every morning, I scroll through my social media. Every morning, I read people arguing against their dehumanisation: because they're Black, because they're LGBTQI, because they're disabled, because they're poor. I recognise the mechanisms and techniques of marginalisation, because so many of them have happened to me. I recognise some of them because, although I like to think I am a good person, as we all like to think we are, I have committed them myself.

There are so many ways of determining that a person isn't fully human, that one person isn't worthy of the same compassion and regard as another. All these mechanisms are deeply interlocked, each into the other, and sometimes they only serve to reinforce the overarching structure: the fight for women's rights reinforces racism, the fight against ableism reinforces sexism, and so on. They're embedded in the very syntax of speech and writing, this language of conquest and assimilation, my native language, English.

Reasons I love English: because it's a language that combines the tactile hardness of Germanic languages with the sensuality of its Latinate roots. As a Mauritian friend, a musician, once said to me: the reason why the French are bad at rock music is because they don't have a word like 'splash'. The English language has edges, hard consonants, the ability to behave like stone. But also: it is fluid, lyric, you can make it as flexible as silk. You can weave with it, chisel with it, stretch it, and distort it, make it bounce, stretch it out, clip it short into aphorisms, make it shout or whisper. It's a language of deep, tactile sensuality.

English has these qualities because it's impure. And it's impure because of empires: the Romans, the Anglo-Saxons, the Normans. And then there was a British Empire, the largest of all the empires there have been in human history, spreading over almost a quarter of the globe: and wherever the English went, they stole words and brought them back home.

Language. A key to freedom. A prison.

Womanhood as we understand it in the Anglo west was invented by men. More, 'woman' is a covertly racial category that applies only to white women (whatever whiteness happens to be in any particular decade, because whiteness is a category of infinite flexibility: it includes and excludes according to its interest). This underpins our thinking so foundationally that Australians commonly claim that the Commonwealth gave the vote to women in 1902, although Aboriginal and Torres Strait Islander women didn't get the vote until 1962, the year I was born.

The Enlightenment was created by a bunch of men who desired freedom for themselves, in their thinking and their lives and their politics. But when women saw the possibility of freedom and equality, those same men did everything they could to limit freedom to men.

The women of the French Revolution rose up and formed the Society of Revolutionary Republican Women, but in October 1793 the Jacobins abolished all the women's clubs and arrested their leaders. In 'Women in Revolution 1789–1796', Olwen Hufton cites the sans-culotte Pierre Gaspard Chaumette, who said when he dissolved the women's clubs that he 'had a right to expect from his wife the running of his home while he attended political meetings: hers was the care of the family: this was the full extent of her civic duties'. When the Napoleonic Code was introduced a decade later, women were given fewer rights than a minor, and the man was legislated as the indisputable leader of the household. The rule of men over women was absolute.

Women, white women, have often replicated this movement, demanding freedom on the one hand and then denying it to others. And always the subordination of a particular category of human beings requires the specification of unique characteristics that in turn justify its inferior status.

Womanhood was made into a special class, and women a special species, to defend us from the dangerous freedom of men. So who is the woman that these men invented?

I have to remind myself that I have no ambition to create a scholarly text in any sense of the word. I lack the training. Not only am I neither a scholar nor a philosopher, I have no wish to be either. Nevertheless ... I find myself mounting arguments. I can't help it.

According to many authorities, I am disqualified before I begin. Nietzsche observed in his 'Apophthegms and Interludes' in *Beyond Good and Evil* that 'When a woman has scholarly inclinations there is generally something wrong with her sexual nature. Barrenness itself conduces to a certain virility of taste; man, indeed, if I may say so, is "the barren animal".' There is nothing wrong with my 'sexual nature', I am far from barren, and I certainly don't aspire to the barrenness of men.

Nevertheless ...

Nietzsche is probably the most intelligent articulator of

contemporary misogyny. He lists nearly all of the shibboleths that Men's Rights Activists repeat ad nauseam on the internet, right down to Milo Yiannopoulos' 'feminism is cancer'.

I reserve scorn for Nietzsche because he opens doors and peeks through them into another possible reality, but hasn't the courage to step over the threshold. Instead, he slams the door shut, and then he nails it up. He sought to undo the binaries of metaphysics in order to discover joy and freedom, but the more he demanded freedom for himself, the liberation from the tired binaries of Good and Evil, the more deeply he had to rift his thought with the oppositional warfare he described between men and women. And the more deeply he imprisoned himself.

Nietzsche is tricky, because so many of the doors that he opens are useful, because his thought is shot through with so many profound perceptions. His writing is reflexive and ambiguous, depending heavily on irony: he is one of the few philosophers I can read, mostly because I so often find him funny. Not always because he intends to be funny, I suspect: but I do. His commentary about women and woman illustrates in an exemplary fashion the double movement of (mostly male) enlightenment — the throwing open of possibilities, only to close off their implications for those whom he'd prefer to keep subordinate and inferior. The wider the possible freedom, the more brutally he must tighten the chains.

'Woman,' he wrote in *Beyond Good and Evil*, 'has so much reason for shame; in woman there is concealed so much superficiality, petty presumption, and petty immodesty.' (Immodesty, from the man who wrote a whole book full of chapters entitled 'Why I Am A Genius'? Ha!) And again: 'What is truth to a woman! From the very first nothing has been more alien, repugnant, inimical to woman than truth — her great art is the lie, her supreme concern is appearance and beauty.' Women are mask, appearance, veils, illusion: woman is deception, and best viewed from a distance.

Woman is not only untruthful, however. Indeed, truth herself might be a woman. It could be that linking women to all that is untruthful and illusory isn't all bad. He writes: 'In spite of all the value which may belong to the true, the positive, and the unselfish, it might be possible that a higher and more fundamental value for life generally should be assigned to pretence, to the will to delusion, to selfishness, and cupidity. It might even be possible that *what* constitutes the value of those good and respected things, consists precisely in their being insidiously related, knotted, and crocheted to these evil and apparently opposed things — perhaps even in being essentially identical with them. Perhaps!'

A glimpse of possibility.

When I first read Nietzsche, I found his desire to invest philosophy with poetic authority both dazzling and profoundly annoying: it seemed to me that doing so changed it into something else. It certainly gave his writing a brilliant, whelming energy. I noted his misogynies, but merely as unfortunate excrescences, rather than as foundational pathologies in his thought. He doesn't mention women often, because his writing exclusively addresses men.

Nevertheless, in all his works, Nietzsche has little good to say about women. Woman is something else: woman is the ideal that man may strive for, the destabiliser in Nietzsche's thought, his weapon against the logic of metaphysics. Woman is truth, the function of morality that he despises. Woman is happiness, which perhaps Nietzsche also despises — he heroicised suffering, which was an invitation to struggle and triumph. And woman is even life itself!

'In the background of all their personal vanity,' he says, 'women themselves have still their impersonal scorn — for "woman".' Indeed. How could we not scorn this 'woman' that men invented for us!

Woman is a different thing from women. Woman is that quality inside women that must be cherished and nurtured so women may fulfil their proper destiny, which is solely to become pregnant, solely to be the 'recreation of the warrior', the chattel of the man who, like the 'Oriental', must possess her. (As always, race nests with sex in the hierarchical categorisation of the value of human beings.)

Then again, there is the wise man in *The Gay Science*:

Someone brought a youth to a wise man and said, 'See, this is one who is being corrupted by women!' The wise man shook his head and smiled. 'It is men,' he called out, 'who corrupt women; and everything that women lack should be atoned for and improved in men, for man creates for himself the ideal of woman, and woman moulds herself according to this ideal.' 'You are too tender-hearted towards women,' said one of the bystanders, 'you do not know them!' The wise man answered: 'Man's attribute is will, woman's attribute is willingness — such is the law of the sexes, verily!

a hard law for woman! All human beings are innocent of their existence, women, however, are doubly innocent; who could have enough of salve and gentleness for them!' 'What about salve! What about gentleness!' called out another person in the crowd, 'we must educate women better!' 'We must educate men better,' said the wise man, and made a sign to the youth to follow him. The youth, however, did not follow him.

And again in *Twilight of the Idols*: 'Man created woman — out of what? Out of a rib of his god — of his "ideal".' Woman is created by man, and that womanhood is miserable for women, 'a hard law'…

It's this insight, that the feminine is created by men, that led some women of his time to embrace his thought, a recognition of a door opening on freedom. Even so, even so: that insight only shines out to be set firmly aside. Freedom was only reserved for the exceptional woman, a woman like Lou Andreas-Salomé, who both helped to articulate Nietzsche's thought and daunted him. Andreas-Salomé knew that her intellectual life was only possible if she sacrificed her sexuality. Her mind, men said, was cold, analytical, male; her male satellites noted that she used 'male' (intellectual), not 'female' (seductive) means to subjugate the world. She was a Pretend-A-Him, one of the most successful of all.

Despite this, her fate was a very feminine one: she is relegated to footnotes in the lives of all the famous men she knew and inspired — Nietzsche, Rilke, Wedekind, Freud. 'The struggle for equal rights,' Nietzsche says in *Ecce Homo*, his final book, 'is even a symptom of disease; every doctor knows this.' In *The Gay Science*, he is more specific:

'The emancipation of women,' — this is the instinctive hatred of physiologically botched — that is to say, barren — women for those of their sisters who are well constituted: the fight against 'man' is always only a means, a pretext, a piece of strategy. By trying to rise to 'Woman *per se*', to 'Higher Woman', to the 'Ideal Woman', all they wish to do is to lower the general level of women's rank: and there are no more certain means to this end than university education, trousers, and the rights of voting cattle.

When Nietzsche considers the impossibility of the notion of equality between men and women, it is because men and women have entirely different ideas about love:

What woman understands by love is clear enough: complete surrender (not merely devotion) of soul and body, without any motive, without any reservation, rather with shame and terror at the thought of a devotion restricted by clauses or associated with conditions. In this absence of conditions her love is precisely a faith: woman has no other. — Man, when he loves a woman, wants precisely this love from her … A man who loves like a woman becomes thereby a slave; a woman, however, who loves like a woman becomes thereby a more perfect woman …

Woman, says Nietzsche, in an insight he probably gained

from Andreas-Salomé, *wants* to be possessed. Moreover, her fidelity goes with this possession, is central to it, whereas for a man, fidelity is a choice, something that may occur as a consequence of his love, but which isn't germane to it. Any woman who attempts to wrest herself out of this condition is, by definition, unwomanly, unnatural. A woman who thinks, says Nietzsche, is by thought alone less womanly. She becomes an abomination, a masculine woman, a beast that is neither one thing nor another. A monster.

This is extremely convenient — or at least, it's convenient for misogynists. And I guess there's a kind of exhilaration in seeing the hatred of women articulated so fundamentally, the foundational senses of it so clearly and unambiguously laid out. It gives something clear to argue against, something that is less like punching mist, which is what arguing misogynies too often feels like, since it constitutes so much of our cultural reality. But there's also a strange sense of vertigo that happens when the very ground of your self is denied existence, when your very life is denied, when you hold up your lived experience only to see it snuffed out in a sophistic dismissal.

It's unsurprising that Nietzsche and August Strindberg, another great modern portraitist of misogyny, admired each other. There's a short fanboy correspondence in which they bond over their mutual hatred of women. 'I read your tragedy [*The Father*] twice with the greatest emotion,' Nietzsche wrote to Strindberg in 1888, when he was beginning to struggle with the insanity that was the final mode of the illness that eventually killed him, syphillis. 'I was astonished beyond all measure to find a work in which my own conception of love — war with regard to its means and in its fundamental laws, nothing less than the deadly hatred of the sexes — had been expressed in so splendid a manner.'

Strindberg was equally pleased with Nietzsche, and tendered some advice on getting his work translated through Europe. He makes an observation that might have surprised my own ancestors, even though Britain was then ruled by a queen: 'With regard to England I have really nothing to say,' wrote Strindberg, 'for there we have to deal with a puritanical land, delivered into the hands of women — which signifies the same thing as having fallen into a state of absolute decadence. English morality — you know what that means, dear sir! Subscription libraries for the young person — Currer Bell, Miss Braddon, and the rest! I advise you to keep clear of all that!'

These two miserable men. I suppose it is some small satisfaction to consider how profoundly they both would have despised the internet, where the clearest reproductions of their grandly proclaimed rancours and resentments now live and breed, slime in a stagnant pond. It's the grist churning in every sweaty little chatroom where men hone their resentment of women, the hatred of the womanness that women possess but do not give or that they throw away, the womanness that is their essential difference, their essential condition of subordination to men.

These two nineteenth-century thinkers are only the articulate edges of divisions that remain embedded deeply in European and US culture, that structure our languages so profoundly that it is almost impossible to think outside them.

The root words that differentiate gender in contemporary English are *man* and *male*: to be a woman, to be female, is merely to be a syllable, an afterthought. The default human body is male, in our language, in our subjectivities. Thus meanings and power relationships are universalised and reinforced through the very language we use and speak.

But it wasn't always so, even in our language. For example: *man* was once a gender-neutral term. It's now beyond reclamation, but there's worth in remembering that man wasn't always the Man, that the Man isn't an eternal verity. In Old English, *man* simply referred to a human being. If you wanted to indicate someone was male, you called him *werman* (*wer* derives from *vir*, the Latin for male). A woman was a *wifman*, which eventually became *wimman*. It still exists in English as both *woman* and *wife*.

It's likewise with *male* and *female*, which despite appearances have entirely separate histories. Male originates from the Latin *mas* or *masculus*, and comes to English via the Old French, *masle*. Female, on the other hand, comes from the Latin *femina* or *femella*, which entered English through the Old French *femelle*. In fourteenth-century England, usage changed *femelle* to *female* to rhyme with *male*. An entire history of female subjecthood was reduced to a mere prefix and along the way, we lost a useful word, man, which meant all of us.

Person, with its syllable *son*, also misleadingly seems to centre the male. Like all our Latinate words, it came into English via the Normans as the Old French *persone*, from the

Latin *persona*, which means both a person and a mask, as was used in Greek and Roman theatres. The OED tracks this from the Latin *personare*, meaning 'to sound through'.

Personhood, the sounds that animate our masked being. The songs of ourselves.

Sisters

What are sisters supposed to be?

Like us? Not like us?

It's probably too easy to overestimate the influence of books: there are so many forces that shape a consciousness. On the other hand, reading formed so much of my mind, then and now: it's part of the direct experience I weave into the ongoing narratives of me. When I read a book as a child, I felt, indefinably but powerfully, that it now belonged to me — more, I felt that in reading it, I had made it part of me. This nudges uncomfortably close to the idea of knowledge as acquisition and colonisation, of the great European libraries full of texts from the conquered worlds. To know has always been too nearly aligned to possession.

This conviction certainly made libraries a difficult proposition: I was always accumulating fines. Even now, our rented house is infeasibly full of books, more than four thousand of them, collecting dust, getting in the way, and almost intolerably burdensome when we have to move house. Every now and then we do a cull, which removes a few boxfuls, but I can't bring myself to get rid of the majority of them. I tell myself that these books are useful, tools of my trade, and this is certainly true, but a library is so many other things. It's memory, biography, a map, a series of personal histories. To get rid of these books would be like deleting some of myself.

I sometimes wonder what it would feel like if the library vanished in some terrible book apocalypse. It might be liberating, a chance to build a new self. It would be devastating. The books are probably the major reason I wish I owned a house, so I would never have to move the books again.

I literally don't know who I would be without books.

Among the books I devoured as a child, there weren't many sets of sisters, and where there were sisters, they almost always had brothers. Like so many other girls, I read and re-read *Little Women*. The tale of the four March sisters, their struggles with each other and themselves, their differences and divisions ameliorated by their underlying love for each other, is one of the ur-stories of modern western sisterhood.

One of the things that most attracted me in *Little Women* was the moral seriousness that underlay their comic misadventures. The March family, creating their selves with true American pragmatism, structured their spiritual aspirations through John Bunyan's Puritan allegory *The Pilgrim's Progress*. I must have been one of the few children my age who read *The Pilgrim's Progress* before I read *Little Women*: we had a nineteenth-century edition that fell victim to my eternal hunger for books. I was fascinated by the engravings: Christian struggling with the weight of his sins and his guilt in the Slough of Despond; or the Celestial City, haloed with a radiance of finely drawn lines, that is his ultimate destination.

I probably read *Little Women* when I was about ten or eleven. I re-read it recently, finding it a rather more eccentric book than I remembered: one of its charms is the space devoted to the Marches' creative lives, their writings and drawings and performances and family societies, which mark major divagations in the narrative. But I was mostly surprised by how much moralising there was — every anecdote is turned to practical illustrative parable, as the endlessly patient and good Marmee models her girls into the little women their father would be proud of, teaching them to fight their 'bosom enemies' — pride, conceit, anger, laziness — and learn the womanly attributes of modesty, sacrifice, and patience.

I'm a bit surprised I wasn't put off by its sometimes saccharine sentimentality, or indeed its insistence that the essence of womanhood is to put aside ego for your man. A woman's mission in life is above all to care for others, to morally shape, chide, and 'manage' others, and to model this behaviour to younger women. Perhaps its idealised picture of family life was a fantasy in which I found comfort, or maybe I simply didn't take much notice of those bits: children are very skilled in editing their reading. What I remembered from the book were all the domestic travails — Amy's humiliation when she brings pickled limes to school, Jo's rage when Amy burns her manuscript and the subsequent drama of remorse and forgiveness, Meg's constant struggle with her vanity and shabby clothes. Naturally, I related most to Jo, the boyish, plain, scruffy wannabe writer; for once, I didn't have to imagine my ambitions into a male protagonist.

Sisters, I thought (if I thought about it at all, which is unlikely: what child thinks about the air it breathes?), are like the Marches: individual, with their own ambitions, but nevertheless implicated deeply in each other, and in the larger project of the family. Despite its profoundly American religiosity, which was deeply foreign, much of *Little Women* was immediately familiar: the absent father, the middle-class struggles with relative poverty, the shabby clothes and social awkwardness. Even their amateur theatricals were familiar: though I had never been to the theatre in my life, we also staged plays for our parents, which I wrote and directed. Actually, it's likely that I've got cause and effect confused here: I probably got the idea for these plays from this and other books. What do we internalise from what we read, what do we merely find expressed there?

Even though I had by then so fiercely rejected Christianity, I was always deeply attracted by moral dramas, the notion of a struggle with oneself, the desire to be 'good'. Maybe it's not odd at all: perhaps the moral stability expressed in such books was an escape from the complexities I had to deal with in my daily life as a teenager. I remember wishing passionately that I could think of my parents as cardboard cut-outs, idealised figures, Mother and Father, who made everything orderly and safe, as opposed to the flawed, vulnerable people I knew they were, whom I was forced to recognise as human, whom I was forced to forgive, because I loved and needed them.

I loved Noel Streatfeild's books about children working in show business, especially the series about the three Fossil sisters, Pauline, Petrova, and Posy, of which the most famous is the much adapted 1936 book *Ballet Shoes*. The series featured a central childhood fantasy (all three children were adopted) and an absent parent, Great-Uncle Matthew (Gum), a geologist and professor who was always overseas. The three children were overseen by their guardian, Sylvia, who was Gum's niece, the disciplinarian Nana, and a sprinkling of female teachers. In fact, these books are almost completely female-centric, which perhaps partly accounts for their enormous popularity.

Noel Streatfeild herself came from a family with four sisters. Born in 1895, she was the second of five surviving children (her younger sister Joyce died of tuberculosis at the age of two). She had a younger brother, William, and her youngest sister, Richenda, was born twenty years after Noel. She was the 'unattractive' girl of the family, as I was. Her novels often feature plain, boyish girls: in *Ballet Shoes*, it's Petrova, who was much more interested in mechanics than in dancing. Like me, Petrova never played with dolls, and like Petrova, I was deeply interested in how machines worked: I took all our alarm clocks to pieces and put them back together again, mostly, and did the same with my Singer sewing machine. Oddly, there was often a mysterious bit left over once I had reassembled these objects, although mainly they seemed to work fine.

If the girls had brothers, even if the girls were active protagonists, the brothers were the leaders. In C.S. Lewis' Narnia books, Lucy and Susan were Queens, but Peter was the High King; if I wanted to be anyone, it was Peter. Lewis' heavy Christian allegorising went right over my head, or maybe, again, I simply ignored it. Even so, even then I felt there was something wrong with the story of Susan, who was banished from Narnia because she was interested in make-up and stockings. When I began to be interested in make-up and stockings myself, I thought of Susan with a pang. It seemed unfair: Peter had grown older, but didn't have to turn into a woman, as Susan did. 'When I was a child, I spake as a child, I understood as a child, I thought as a child: but when I became a man, I put away childish things,' said Saint Paul. But only a man could put away childish things: to become a grown-up woman was to be exiled from heaven.

Other stories I remember: E. Nesbit's *The Railway Children*, set against the background of the 1904 Russo-Japanese War, in which three children and their writer mother moved from their comfortable middle-class home in London to a country house in Yorkshire after the father was unjustly accused of spying and sent to prison. This was another family of three, and Bobbie, the oldest, always touched me: she was, unlike her younger siblings, privy to her mother's secret grief. As I was, so often, before my mother left.

I particularly loved Monica Dickens' World's End series, because the four children living by themselves on a ramshackle farm with dozens of animals were so familiar. We had as many animals as we could look after. There were cats, dogs, rabbits, guinea pigs, cows, calves, horses, and a succession of baby magpies that we raised after saving them from becoming road-kill. Once, with our substitute cousins, who also had guinea pigs, we entered our pet rodents in the Melbourne Show. I still remember our pride as we went through the turnstiles with our exhibitor passes. We built show cages out of fruit boxes, painting them black outside and white inside, as per the instructions, only to find that they were a couple of centi-metres too big. The show organisers were kind, and no doubt amused, and gave us standard cages for free. Between us, we won some rosettes, and my sister's guinea pig bit the judge.

Fairytales: Cinderella with her three ugly sisters and wicked stepmother and she the beautiful mistreated princess (we were all mistreated princess and ugly sister in turn, all longing for our fairy godmother to arrive and dispense justice, to take us to the ball). Snow White and Snow Red, the two good sisters who were visited by a bear who turned out to be a prince under an enchantment. Christina Rossetti's 'Goblin Market'.

I'm not sure what they added up to, these books. Those I liked best and returned to most often were books where children were self-sufficient, where they were portrayed as capable and independent, as agents in their lives. Irreparable breaches seldom happened: the only one I can think of was Susan, banished from heaven. Mostly when a child betrayed the others, as Edmund did in *The Lion, the Witch, and the Wardrobe*, or when Amy burned Jo's manuscript, there was forgiveness and redemption: the quarrel taught the children something about themselves and each other.

Only fairytales held those darker secrets: the ugly sisters cutting off their toes to fit the glass slipper; the wicked queen demanding the heart of Snow White, forced to wear a pair of red-hot shoes and dance in them until she died. The less-realist stories expressed the more uncomfortable truths.

Two things, nevertheless, are very clear: almost all these books, like the generality of twentieth-century children's stories in English, are middle-class. Where there are working-class characters, they figure as servants like Hannah, the devoted live-in housekeeper in *Little Women*, who is considered part of the family, always cooks Christmas dinner, but never sits at the table; or as functionaries like the Porter in *The Railway Children*. And without exception, the protagonists are all profoundly white.

From about the age of seven, I was fiercely atheist. I 'tested' God, daring Him to exist — strange, irrational tests. I remember one: I told myself that if I touched a certain banner during a school church service, and nothing happened, then God wasn't real. There was probably some kind of proof he had to manifest. The banner was a long stretch out of the chapel pew, and I still remember the girl next to me asking what I was doing. The gesture for me was imbued with dreadful significance. What if something did happen? What if I were punished for daring God? But my neighbour's puzzlement and my embarrassment were the only results: I touched the banner, and nothing happened, as I had known nothing would. God was a fraud.

Christianity started falling apart for me a little earlier, in England, when I was about five. One of our spaniels was run over outside our front gate. I remember my father bringing her body up the path, blood on his arms, to be buried in the garden. I asked if she would go to heaven and he said, no, animals didn't go to heaven. This made absolutely no sense to me: if I had a soul, then how was it possible that animals didn't? What use was a God who said animals had no souls, when so plainly they loved and played and suffered like we did?

I guess I felt this strongly because my first language was dog. I ran around with my mother's great danes and barked, long before I said any human words. I was one of those children who spoke late, and when I started speaking, did so in complete sentences. I guess I held my own counsel from the beginning.

Once I was certain God was a fairy story, only as real as all the other fairy stories I read and loved, I was pretty sure everyone else was lying about religion. I was sure that they knew as well as I did that it was all a big pretence; I was privately scornful that anyone could believe in a God who took a personal interest in their affairs, a God that was *obviously* a fantasy that was at best a blanket to make people feel better about living in a world that was without justice, or at worst a threatening authority figure who was a proxy for earthly punishment and control.

It was strange later to realise that Christianity, perhaps filtered through the allegorical stories I inhaled as a child, formed the ethical imagination of my adulthood. Notions such as not doing harm to others or being truthful aren't specific to Christianity, but there's no denying that my ideas were in a Christian shape. Even now that passage from Corinthians has the power to stir me: 'And now abide faith, hope, love, these three; but the greatest of these is love.'

When I grasped how much Christianity infuses my imagination, I began to wonder what else I had absorbed along the way: the evil, power-hungry, sensual Calormenes in the Narnia books must surely have conditioned my orientalism as much as anything in my family history. It wasn't that Black people weren't represented in our library: they were present, as they had to be present, as part of the patrimony of the British Empire. All these representations were racist: Enid Blyton's golliwogs, *Little Black Sambo*. There was an illustrated book from South Africa about 'piccaninnies', which I remember in no detail, and an edition of the Uncle Remus stories about Br'er Rabbit, which I adored for their trickster hero, who was always at odds with his nemeses, Br'er Bear and Br'er Fox.

I think this book came from the Hollies, my father's childhood house in Grampound. First published in 1881, they were folk tales collected by a white journalist, Joel Chandler Harris, from African American slaves who worked on a plantation in the Deep South. They're written in a representation of the Black dialect at the time, and set on a slave plantation.

In her fascinating book *Racial Innocence: performing*

American childhood from slavery to civil rights, Robin Bernstein says that Harris is 'one of slavery's most effective and influential apologists', who 'influenced writers from Mark Twain to Rudyard Kipling to Beatrix Potter'.

Nothing is innocent, not even Peter Rabbit.

Bernstein explores the links between the seven Uncle Remus books and *Uncle Tom's Cabin*, which Harris called 'a wonderful defence of slavery', appropriating and inverting Harriet Beecher Stowe's anti-slavery message. 'For Harris, the "real moral that Mrs Stowe's book teaches is that the ... realities [of slavery], under the best and happiest of conditions, possess a romantic beauty and a tenderness all their own."' Harris identified with the 'Lost Cause' of the antebellum South, a nostalgia for a uniquely chivalrous and noble civilisation that is now lost. 'To be a postwar white southerner who subscribed to Lost Cause ideology, as Harris was and did, meant to consider oneself a victim who had been stripped of the "right" to own slaves, a refugee from a noble and ruined civilization.' Bernstein describes a 'self-perception of victimhood' that is very familiar in the nationalistic, white-supremacist right-wing ideology all too ubiquitous now.

The figure of Uncle Remus is drawn as a picture of the innocence of slavery. In the opening chapter of the first book, he is introduced with a small white boy on his lap whom he is enchanting with his stories. The boy is staring with 'intense interest into the rough, weather-beaten face, that beamed so kindly upon him'. In a later book, the descendent of that little boy, a product of the post–Civil War period, is portrayed as effeminate, 'fragile' and 'polite'. When he too meets Uncle

Remus, he reproduces the pose, but Remus can't really reach him because the 'trouble with the boy was that he had no childhood'. 'The "childhood" that this boy lacked,' Bernstein goes on to say, 'was not a biological state of development, but the historical experience of plantation slavery … Harris and other plantation writers succeeded in mapping the Lost Cause upon what Carolyn Steedman calls the "lost realm" of childhood: he hitched nostalgia for plantation slavery to nostalgia for childhood; thus he made slavery seem innocent.'

What makes these tales particularly egregious is that their major charm — the funny stories about how Br'er Rabbit tricks and outwits his enemies — are all appropriated from the African Americans that Harris is condemning to slavery.

I had no idea about any of the context, but I loved Br'er Rabbit. It's impossible to think that Harris' racism didn't enter my head in some way as unconscious confirmation of what every other book I read also told me: that only white people, like me, could be protagonists, that people of colour existed only to serve us.

Our family didn't know anyone who wasn't white. Even in South Africa, I have no memory of anyone who was Black, although I must have gone through the streets with my mother, I must have encountered the maids who worked in our house. The country town where I lived from seven to fifteen was one of the whitest towns in Australia, until recently mostly insulated from the huge migrations that mark the Australian population. Like other towns in country Victoria, it boasted the single Chinese restaurant, the Mee Hing, where we went for treats: Fanta, and deep-fried sweet-and-sour chicken. My best friend at school, Anna, whose parents had fled the war in Cyprus, ran a milk bar where I sometimes helped to serve customers. Even in 2011, when it was immeasurably more cosmopolitan than it had been in the seventies, when I lived there, only 8 per cent of the population was born overseas — compared with 24.6 per cent nationwide — and more than half of those came from northern Europe.

All these divagations: it's as if my thinking skates off, glancing away from the painfulness of our sisterhood.

I lost faith, hope, and love — even the greatest of these three. My entire ethical system failed.

Our mother was the cherished only girl in her family: letters from her father are rich with endearments, 'my darling precious girl'. Perhaps, despite her real attempts to be fair to each of us, there could only be one precious girl, one special darling. Throughout our childhood, that was our youngest sister.

My sister and I banded together to bitch about that. It was the jealousy of the older children for the indulged youngest, the child who had it easier than us. I had my own complaints about being the oldest of all, the child who had to be 'responsible', the child who wasn't allowed to be silly, whose behaviour was expected to model adulthood to her siblings. It felt so deeply unfair.

All those childish injustices, which at the time felt like weals across the soul. 'Life is unfair, dear.' Whose turn was it to do the washing-up? Why was I being told to do it twice in a row? Why did this sister get a special treat and not me? Why did the other child get a present when it was *my* birthday? When we were given lollies, we distributed them with acute precision, each of us watching like hawks, into three piles. We jealously tracked the distribution of privileges: if one child lucked out, we others felt it as a personal insult, an imbalance in the cosmos.

Children behave like this from a very early age; a sense of fairness, or unfairness at unjust treatment, is innate. Sometimes, if I happen to be outside and the cat is locked indoors, she wails in fury through the window, although she is perfectly content when everyone is inside the kitchen. A wide area of research has observed empathy or a sense of social right and wrong in animals, from rats to birds to elephants: animals play, analyse and solve problems, grieve, show and demand affection, communicate with each other. Like us, they are individual beings that exist in social contexts. The fairytales about animals that can speak are only partly anthropomorphic: anyone who watches animals for any length of time sees these behaviours. A child, or certainly the child that was me, doesn't perceive a great deal of difference between themselves and any animal they know.

Professor Frans de Waal, a primate behaviourist at Emory University, Atlanta, Georgia, told *The Telegraph* that animals do share many human psychological behaviours. 'I don't believe animals are moral in the sense we humans are — with well developed and reasoned sense of right and wrong,' he said, 'rather that human morality incorporates a set of psychological tendencies and capacities such as empathy, reciprocity, a desire for co-operation and harmony that are older than our species. Human morality was not formed from scratch, but grew out of our primate psychology. Primate psychology has ancient roots, and I agree that other animals show many of the same tendencies and have an intense sociality.'

I believed that from toddlerhood, when I talked to dogs. It's why I feel — so many of us feel — the mass extinctions perpetrated by modern capitalism as much more than a question of destroying our own homes. It's a mass killing that parallels and complements the countless genocides of empire: the darkening of uncounted billions of lives is a grief beyond expression, a suffering beyond measurement, an injustice beyond reparation.

But here I am, spiralling out again. Relationships are so complicated, they reach out into ever-widening ecologies, they spiral in to the most minute trackings of consciousness. You tug at one tiny strand and the whole web begins to tremble.

Trauma distorts our selves: it warps memory and experience. I know this has happened to me. And to my sisters.

My sister's trauma grew into an unannealed sense of grievance, a heightened belief in her unquestionable rightness against the wrongs, real or imagined, that are perpetrated against her. Our childhoods were full of wrongs, large and small, but we all suffered them. In our adulthoods, how we dealt with them seemed to diverge: those childish quarrels seem now to me to be so much the result of our childish unhappiness. For all of us were, in our different ways, unhappy. I am able to forgive our childish selves; I can forgive the confused, damaged people we were in our twenties. How could we not fuck up?

She has forgiven me nothing, not the smallest transgression.

Why do I believe, somewhere in the centre of my being, that women shouldn't abandon each other, that there is such a thing as the sisterhood? We betray each other all the time.

Many second-generation western feminists parsed the nature/nurture division as respectively sex and gender: sex was the body you were born with, gender its social expression. This permitted the creation of women as a class defined by their bodies, and subjected to a unique series of social oppressions. As with all the binaries, this is a damaging reduction of a vastly complicated reality. Very little has been more disturbing to me in the past decade than watching the rise of transphobic feminism, seeing feminists joining hands with the conservative right, policing bodies with the enthusiasm of a fundamentalist evangelical preacher.

Up until a decade or so ago, I had always assumed that, as a social-justice movement, feminism was profoundly concerned with justice. It was a major shock to discover feminisms that are as repressive and vicious as the patriarchal structures they seek to combat, that generate their existence through a policy of paranoid borders. But that was simply my ignorance: since the beginnings of feminism, there have always been activists who only fought for the rights of *some* women. Angela Davis, among others, recorded how the US suffrage movement, which initially had strong ties to the movement for racial emancipation, consciously decided to renounce the struggle against Black slavery. But there's more to the darkness in feminism than base pragmatism.

Some of feminism's most famous advocates were deeply racist. The transphobic, racist feminists who ally themselves with Christian conservatives are not exceptions. As Emmeline Pankhurst, the famous suffragette, shows, they're practically traditional.

The Pankhurst family is fascinating, a kind of activist parallel to the Mitford family. The Mitford girls split four ways: Unity became a Nazi and a friend of Hitler, and shot herself when Britain declared war on Germany. Jessica became a socialist and went to fight in the Spanish Civil War. Diana, a society beauty, married the heir to the Guinness fortune. And Nancy became a writer. The Pankhursts also split along lines that seem to reflect the divisions of the twentieth century: after the outbreak of World War I, Adela and Sylvia became socialists and communists, while their mother, with their sister Christabel, became fierce defenders of the empire.

Emmeline was the increasingly autocratic leader of the Women's Social and Political Union, of which her daughters Sylvia and Christabel were both members. (Sylvia, an artist who studied at the Manchester School of Art and later at the Royal School of Art, designed the WSPU's logos and banners.) The WSPU campaigned for the vote for women, and gradually pursued a course of increasing militancy, from breaking windows and burning 'women's votes' into golf courses with acid, to setting fire to buildings: an orchid house in Kew Gardens, pillar boxes, and a railways carriage. This militancy alienated many of their allies. All the Pankhursts were arrested, imprisoned, and force-fed multiple times.

On the outbreak of World War I, Emmeline and Christabel announced that 'as Suffragists we could not be pacifists at any price'. They formed the Women's Party, a militantly xenophobic pro-war group that, among other things, handed out white feathers to shame conscientious objectors. The Women's Party campaigned for equal pay, equal marriage and divorce laws, maternity and infant care, and a number of other feminist issues. They also campaigned for the abolition of trade unions, and pursued a virulent anti-immigration agenda. Emmeline and Christabel were lauded by the Tory press for their patriotism.

Meanwhile, Christabel's sisters Sylvia and Adela campaigned for peace, Sylvia in Britain and Adela in Australia, where she was working against the introduction of conscription. Sylvia, a socialist and peace activist who organised with working-class women and was a vocal protester of imperialism and racism, faced constant vilification, and was pelted with rotten fruit by angry soldiers.

Emmeline eventually joined the Conservative Party. It's surprising, in retrospect, that Margaret Thatcher refused the label of feminism: Emmeline was her perfect precursor.

Adela's story is as confounding as her mother's. She was a founding member of the Communist Party of Australia. In 1927, after she was expelled from the CPA, she was one of the founding members of the anti-communist Australian Women's Guild of Empire and, in 1941, the fascist Australia First Movement, which promoted alliance with the Axis powers. Other members were the writers Xavier Herbert, Miles Franklin, and Eleanor Dark. I sometimes wonder why nobody remembers that these hallowed names of Australian literature were apologists for fascism.

Sylvia, on the other hand, remained anti-fascist and anti-colonialist for the rest of her life. She was an avid supporter of Emperor Haile Selassie of Ethiopia, campaigning against the Italian invasion of Ethiopia, and after 1956 moved to Addis Ababa with her son. A blog post by development economist Owen Barder that records a memorial service on the fiftieth anniversary of her death notes that she is the only foreigner buried in the space at Holy Trinity Cathedral reserved for patriots of the Italian war. Sylvia is also often called the 'forgotten Pankhurst', although on that same blog post, a commenter called Misgan Lemi says touchingly: 'We Ethiopian love her forever ... she was rational, objective person, pronounced humanity ... her ideology lives eternal even if she died ...'

Empire writes itself into our bones. There's no escaping our reckoning with it. Either we remake ourselves from the ground up, or we become its avatars.

While the Pankhursts seem to map in their personal relation-ships the global and ideological conflicts of the twentieth century, it's not so in our family. We're at the petty edge of those same conflicts, with smaller understandings, smaller passions.

Maybe our biographies reflect how these larger patterns became internalised, atomised, individualised. How difficult it became to link the self to larger movements as the twentieth century moved into the twenty-first. How the self became privatised. How it became a commodity.

The labyrinth

I read an essay by Sunny Singh, 'The Gait of the Elephant'. She writes about using the language of the conqueror, of negotiating the endless fractures of empire through the endless lateral violence it imposes. She speaks of discovering a 'language of liberation', a 'language of revolution'. She writes:

> One night, hurt and exhausted, I make a list of things I want to hear, of questions I want to ask, of answers I want to seek and learn: are we irreparably broken by our histories, especially since so many of us have been and still are weaponized against each other? Can we become friends when equality remains a dream even amongst those of us who look similar? Can we be lovers when we have been taught to fear and envy and hate each other and ourselves? Where can desire take seed when our brown and black bodies are negated and abnegated? Can we ever

find ways to negotiate the many webs of dispossession and marginalization, of colour and shape and desires and histories? How can we rebuild ourselves or forge our futures when we are so angry and afraid and yet direct our frustrations at each other?

Are we irreparably broken by our histories? I recognise this question, even if my body is marked white: the price of empire was always doing to our psyches, willingly, what we did violently to the unwilling bodies of others.

I feel as if, writing this, I am trying to write my way towards the same decolonised space from the opposite end: an inheritor of the conquerors, who speaks, who *loves*, the conquerors' language. I tell Sunny this, confessing my doubts. 'It will be useful,' she tells me. 'Decolonisation isn't just for the former colonies. Brexit is the coloniser slashing and burning and self-destroying because it refuses to acknowledge history. Maybe if more white Britons wrote from the decolonising side, it would have been different.'

There is a truth in this, and I am a little comforted. But I know I must keep this question foregrounded, this doubt alive and sharp. It is too easy to presume.

My people have always presumed.

I think of how German officers responsible for killing Jews were told it was noble to overcome their natural human compassion in order to rid the world of the Jewish infection. It was part of the struggle, to overcome this weakness, to learn how to kill without compunction. To numb that part of themselves.

Japanese soldiers were trained to use the bayonet with living prisoners of war. I think of a horrifying documentary on the Rape of Nanking in which one soldier admitted no revulsion, no repentance, about the horrors and atrocities committed then, because he enjoyed it. He was a psychopath. These people are very useful in war and business. But those who are not psychopathic must, in the serving of empire, become so.

The Anglo empire as we know it — Britain, the United States, they are both the same, one the inheritor of the other, Trump himself no less crude and cruel and avaricious than Robert Clive and the East India Company — is a psychopathic machine. There are other empires, rising and falling, flexing their muscles in the twilight of European capitalism. China, India, Japan, Russia. Each of them has its own imperial atrocities. But in the past half-millennium, the empire of Anglo whiteness has most wounded our world.

It's also the empire on which I can speak with most authority, as I peer through the tiny letterbox that frames my view of the world.

My family, the foot soldiers of empire, lowly and high. My Cornish father married my mother and took her out to South Africa because the best way to make money as a young man was to work in the goldmines.

A.L. Rowse observes that it was a common thing when he was young to meet Cornishmen who had travelled to South Africa or America, but who had never visited the neighbouring village five miles away. My family's biography was more than an individual knot in the weave. It's an imperial biography, a colonial biography: the sons ventured out into the colonies, to Malaya, to Canada, to Australia, to wrest riches from the breast of the earth and bring them home.

As a child, I never thought about what that meant. In England, we lived an orderly life in that beautiful Georgian farmhouse as my father travelled the world, sending back postcards that we pasted into a scrapbook: 3D images of Disney characters that you could tilt to make things move, beaten copper postcards from Chile. I had no reason to think about it. It was just how things were.

My father subscribed to a monthly magazine called *Pictorial Knowledge*. When I google it, I find Newnes' *Pictorial Knowledge*, which dates from the 1930s, but no sign of the bright-orange volumes we gathered in the 1970s, magazine by monthly magazine, carefully filed in ringbinders to build up to an encyclopaedia. I read each magazine from cover to cover. It had articles about history, science, medicine, astronomy, art. *Pictorial Knowledge* was where I first read about the rhyming pattern of a Shakespearean sonnet, abab, cdcd, efef, gg. I wrote one myself, the first formal poem I remember consciously writing.

It was where I first read, when I was probably about ten years old, about King Leopold II's crimes in the Belgian Congo. There was a photograph of a man whose arm had been hacked off. You could still see where the blade had cut, like you might see slices in a tree. It was one of the pictures to which I often returned, like Goya's painting of *Saturn*

Devouring His Son or a painting of Crusaders baptising infidel babies in Jerusalem so their souls would fly to heaven when the men slaughtered them. These were all pictures that filled me with a cold horror, that such things could be.

In *Pictorial Knowledge*, there was a map of the British Empire, the whole world filled with pink. I remember believing that the British Empire, unlike the monstrous Belgian Congo or the cruel Spanish Conquistadors, was kindly and just. The British brought enlightenment, order, and railways. We brought the English language, with its freight of culture, with its Shakespeare and Bible. The British brought adulthood to the childish natives, who otherwise wouldn't know how to run things.

I never questioned the place of these received truths. They were part of the texture of how things were. I was English, so I wanted to believe that my family was different from King Leopold II, who chopped the arms off children. Even when I began to question my family myths, I still held, underneath all my conscious thoughts, these rags of unquestioning faith. It was as if there were an invisible field that forbade interrogation.

It can take a lifetime to undo the things you were born with. Even as I rebelled, even as I rejected my mother's drillings of femininity and manners, even as I began to speak with an Australian accent, even after my grandmother turned around in her kitchen and spat at me, 'You're not British!' … even then, I was still haunted by these ghosts. The language I speak and write in, the culture that shaped me, the passport that still classifies me as a British citizen. How long does it take to ask questions, if what you are questioning is the very fibre of who you are?

Too long. Way too long.

I'm not interested in writing a mea culpa. I'm not interested in throwing ashes on my head and throwing myself on the ground in penitence. I'm not interested in displays of my guilt or my culpability. Take this as read: I was raised in a racist, sexist, hierarchical culture, and just as I had to learn (am still learning) how to undo all the prohibitions imposed by the patriarchs, rows and rows of them in their robes like in the medieval paintings, leading all the way up to the Throne of God, so I am learning to unlearn racism.

It's useful for me to look at the threads that draw together in my life, tracing them back and back through generations, attempting to make these invisible things visible, interrogatable. I don't know how useful this would be for anyone else; these threads, these shapings, are painfully visible to anyone born outside the imprimatur of whiteness. I'm back stating the obvious, again. Sometimes I think it's the only thing I really do.

I need these narratives that give me a larger picture of who I am. I think all human beings do. Sometimes we need comfort, sometimes we need a sense of purpose, sometimes we just need to know that we are not alone or that we belong somewhere. Sometimes we just want to find out what went wrong. We want to know how we fit, where we fit. We like to think that we are part of something that is larger than ourselves. But stories are so dangerous, especially when they constitute the unconscious scaffolding of the self, when they are grown so ubiquitous and large that they obscure our view.

Our family's biggest story, the told and the untold, was the British Empire. It took me a lot longer to see through Britishness than it did to see through God. My family wasn't especially religious: we went to church occasionally, and although we were sent to Church of England schools, that was a decision that was more about class than religion. When I started school in England, I went to the state primary school, Carclaze in St Austell, but when we moved to Australia, it was Queen's Church of England Girls' Grammar School in Ballarat, with its grey straw boater hats and gloves, because those schools were 'better'. They were more English, perhaps. Being English was 'better'. My mother drilled us in the proper pronunciation of words, so the 'right people' would recognise us, when we went back 'home'. It was very important that we didn't catch those vulgar colonial accents.

I can only write my own story, but how is this not the same story that has been told, over and over again, at the expense of so many other stories? How is this not the story of the conquerors?

(There is no answer to this one.)

(And yet … I too have been silenced.)

Perhaps there is a value in unpicking the idea of 'innocence'.

From birth, I was steeped in the taken-as-read innocence of the British Empire. The empire that had no ill-intentions, that was superior, civilised, orderly. The innocence I see written all over the United States, that same innocence that cannot reckon with its history of slavery and dispossession, its present of cruelty. And here, in Australia, that same innocence in the face of the most comprehensive robbery of a people of their land and their culture and their lives.

As Alexis Wright says in an essay in *Meanjin*, for First Nations people in Australia, 'the powerful spirits of our ancestral homeland [are] imbued in the soul of our people, who are country itself'. This, she says, is where 'true sovereign governance' exists. In erasing Indigenous sovereignty over their land, the legacy of terra nullius erases the sovereignty of First Nations peoples over their very being — and in doing this, it erases their very humanity.

I was beginning to get a clue, but only partly, when the Port Arthur massacre happened in 1996. By then, I had been trained as a journalist. I picked up the newspapers (we still read newspapers back then) and recoiled at the headlines: THE DEATH OF INNOCENCE.

Port Arthur was one of the worst punishment camps in the gulag that was early colonial Australia. It was patently absurd to claim that Port Arthur, a museum to these very crimes, was a place of peace and tranquillity. It seemed to me typical of the erasures of Australian history. I was correct to think this. But even then, I didn't think past what the English colonists did to their own. I didn't think about the Frontier Wars, the genocidal campaigns against the Lia Pootah and Palawa people on the island of Tasmania, the destruction of their languages and culture, the massacres and betrayals and rapes that constructed Van Diemen's Land. I didn't think about the erasures that this colonial system of punishment and slavery was part of, that my presence here in this unceded land is still a part of.

I didn't know. But as judges say when sentencing, ignorance is no excuse.

Clinging to the cooler edge

Things move too fast. As the New Year opened for 2020, I sat and watched as the country burned, as people posted photographs of eerily crimson hellscapes. A masked child on a boat off Mallacoota, looking back over their burning home. The sun in Sydney, a red eye burning through bushfire smoke. Headlines saying that a billion animals had burned to death. Breathing in the ash of ancient forests, dead animals, the homes of the lost.

2020 already was too much and then by March we were in lockdown for the pandemic. Flood, fires, pandemic. Like so many disasters, from the shift in our climate to the escalations that followed the invasion of Iraq, these were disasters that had been predicted for years. We watched like Cassandra as death rained down from the skies, our voices silenced, the lie machine revving up with one more conspiracy theory.

The only prize for being right is this endless grief.

—

Thinking back, 2019 almost seems benign. I was dreading the coming summer, feeling it unfurling through the dry winter like a slow apocalypse. But down in the south, it was merciful. I thought it must be because of the cooling air floating north from the melting ice sheets of Antarctica.

It wasn't so for the rest of Australia, which was baking. It's now so common for temperature records to be broken that we don't even take notice anymore. I stared at the daily weather maps, a swathe of deep red, orange, black, purple. The Bureau of Meteorology introduced purple as a new temperature colour in 2013 to indicate extreme heat: it's surprising how quickly it became normal to see swatches of purple across the centre of the map, the burning continent fading to yellows at the coast.

I deal as well with heat as most northern Europeans — which is to say, not very well. My pale, freckled skin is getting old, and a country childhood completely free of sunblock means that already I'm having lesions removed, new scars among the old. Our shabby old weatherboard rental didn't have built-in aircon, the new indicator of class division; after two days in the high thirties, the heat became inescapable. We kept a portable air conditioner in the old part of the house, which stayed cooler because of the high ceilings.

I'd already mapped my strategies. There was a modern library down the road, with a room full of desks where I could plug in my laptop. Our favourite cinema was only four suburbs away down the train line, and sometimes we went to watch a movie during the hottest part of the day. Always the longer movies. But we only had a single day over forty degrees. We cling to the cooler edge of a burning continent.

Every day, literally every day, I read stories about environmental apocalypse. The rapidly heating ocean, where fish will become extinct by 2046. The disappearing insects. Fruit bats falling dead out of trees. The destruction of the Murray-Darling river system, which drains about one-seventh of the Australian landmass, traditional home of many Aboriginal nations. Some are listed as advisors on the Murray-Darling Basin Authority.

I read the names of the different Aboriginal peoples: in the north, the Barkindji (Paakintji), Barunggam, Bidjara, Bigambul, Budjiti, Euahlayi, Gamilaroi, Githabul, Gunggari, Gwamu (Kooma), Jarowair, Kambuwal, Kunja, Kwiambul, Maljangapa, Mandandanji, Mardigan, Murrawarri, Ngemba, Ngiyampaa, Wailwan, and Wakka Wakka; in the south, the Barapa Barapa, Barkindji, Dhudhuroa, Dja Dja Wurrung, Latji Latji, Maraura, Mutti Mutti, Nari Nari, Ngarrindjeri, Ngintait, Nyeri Nyeri, Tatti Tatti, Taungurung, Wadi Wadi, Wamba Wamba, Waywurru, Wegi Wegi, Wergaia, Wiradjuri, Wolgalu, Wotjobaluk, Yaitmathang, Yita Yita, and Yorta Yorta.

On Wikipedia, it says that the Maraura resisted settlement and were mostly wiped out in a series of killings, including the 1841 Rufus River massacre by South Australian police that was led by sub-inspector Bernard Shaw, South Australia's protector of Aborigines.

According to Robert Lindsay in the Australian Dictionary of Biography, the Aboriginal leader Nanya was a Maraura of the lower Darling who watched as a child as his people were murdered. In 1860, when he would have been in his mid-twenties, he left his camp with two women and went into the arid mallee country between the Darling Anabranch and the South Australian border, known as the 'Scotia blocks', where he lived for over thirty years. In the early 1890s, they were 'rescued', persuaded to return to the camp.

'Rescued'.

The family was tracked down by three Aboriginal stockmen, Harry Mitchell, Dan McGregor, and Fred Williams. According to the rescuers' descendents, the stockmen were worried that the family might be shot by settlers. Given this, there's an odd sentence in the entry: 'White settlers, previously indifferent, became anxious for the family's, and their own, welfare.' It's a strange doublespeak, in which the truth peeps through a statement that at once acknowledges settler paranoia (the 'wild tribe' posed a threat to settler safety) and insists on settler innocence. Nanya's family were brought back to civilisation *for their own good*, out of altruistic concern for their welfare.

The old story.

The biographer notes that while they were in good health when they arrived, the women rapidly 'became stout on a diet of flour and sugar'. The entry ends with this coda:

Many of his children, with no acquired resistance to introduced disease, died soon after their isolation ended. In 1905 his son Billy, educated for a time in Adelaide, was being transferred by the paddle-steamer Gem to Point McLeay mission, on Lake Alexandrina. Tormented to desperation by crew-members, Billy jumped into the steamer's engine and was cut to pieces.

'Rescue'. The torsion of that word. I see the same torsion in the language used on the reassuring, authoritative website of the Murray-Darling Basin Authority (banner government-blue, sober, a photograph of a thriving river landscape). 'The Murray-Darling Basin Authority,' the major tagline says, 'aims to achieve a healthy working Basin for the benefit of all Australians.' There are charts and data, which I have an idle look at, not being equipped to understand what they mean, although I notice much of the 'latest data' on water flow is marked 'not measured'.

In the newspaper, I read how Menindee Lake has been drained twice in the past four years so the MDBA can claim the resulting reduction in water evaporation as part of its 'water savings', even though scientists have told them of the harm it will do. Has done. Is doing.

The Murray-Darling river system, the website cheerily tells me, is also home to hundreds of species of animals. I read down the list, wondering how many more are endangered or extinct since the webpage was last updated. '367 species of birds (35 endangered), which include 98 species of waterbirds; 85 species of mammals (20 extinct, 16 endangered); 46 species of native fish; 53 species of native frogs; 46 species of snakes (5 endangered); 100 species of lizards (1 endangered); 3 species of freshwater turtles; 124 families of macroinvertebrates.'

On the internet, a fish kill went viral: millions of fish suffocated in the water, some of them Murray cod that were more than a century old. Angry farmers were videoed holding the giant dead fish in their arms, crying. I stared at a photograph of a doomed kangaroo in the cracked bed of Menindee Lake, the animal pushing through the mud, its eyes staring with thirst.

When I was a child, I was haunted by a photograph in *Pictorial Knowledge* of a field of mud patterned with endless cracks. That was the only picture that I had seen of Australia before I came here, and I thought it was all like that. There was no perspective in the photograph, so they could have been giant cracks, I could fall through them into the darkness, into the centre of the earth. I had nightmares about it.

The nightmares are coming true.

It wasn't because of the drought, people say of the Murray-Darling. It was because a cotton farm stole the equivalent of four Sydney Harbour's worth of water from the system, leaving everyone downstream, animals, humans, to die of thirst. The Murray-Darling Basin Royal Commission's senior counsel, Richard Beasley SC, concluded, a month before the commission was due to report its findings, that 'The implementation of the Basin Plan has been marred by mal-administration. By that I mean mismanagement by those in charge of the task in the Basin Authority, its executives and its board, and the consequent mismanagement of huge amounts of public funds.' It's couched in the restrained, careful language of law. One more governmental betrayal in a history of unconscionable betrayals.

Journalists discuss the drought as if that catastrophe were 'natural' and the mismanagement was the telling point. But the drought isn't 'natural' either. We all know that the rising temperatures are what human beings have done. The energy and mining companies understood very well — as early as the 1950s — what would happen if they kept pulling oil and coal out of the planet's surface and pumping its carbon into the atmosphere. The agricultural industry knows what will happen with its millions of monocultured hectares, where nothing can live except what is put there; it knows what will happen if we keep pumping factory farmed animals with antibiotics; it knows what pesticides do to insect populations.

They know: they need that knowledge in order to counter the arguments of environmentalists, to damp down the daily observations of gardeners in Cornwall, reporting that daffodils are opening two months earlier than ever before, of farmers who tap their rain gauges and compare the results to records they have kept for decades and shake their heads. The companies need to know so they can bulldoze the knowledge of Indigenous people, land protectors, water protectors, who have cared for this earth for thousands of years, who see their sacred places gutted and poisoned by mines, burned to ash, flooded, destroyed for a new freeway.

I don't understand how you can know these things and still decide to destroy this world. There are people who simply deceive themselves, or who are deceived — but there are also people who coldly, deliberately, in full knowledge of the facts, decide that the 'price' is 'worth it'.

I don't understand it. But also, I do.

Sometimes it's hard to perceive what's obvious. Then again, the colonial project is almost wholly about ensuring that the obvious cannot be seen; it's a process of obfuscation and libel and lies, a global project of gaslighting entire peoples. The British, I was told all my young life, 'helped the natives'. We came to these dark countries out of the goodness of our hearts to bring the Light of Civilisation. It was obvious that we brought subjugation, misery, destruction, and death — my ancestors couldn't have looked at the people we subjugated without seeing that, surely? But the colonial project demanded that we see this as improvement, and so, obediently, we did: misery and enslavement were redefined as the process of civilisation, as the necessities of moral and cultural improvement. If those we 'rescued' died of disease or ill-treatment, like Nanya's family, it was a footnote, an unfortunate result of their inability to adapt. Even if they were 'rescued' from our own violence, their 'rescue' was an expression of our 'concern'.

It takes a lot of energy to conceal the obvious. It takes centuries of conditioning to make it seem natural that sticking a flag in some soil means that 'we' own a continent. But the first duty of empire, as the English Crown noted of those who were 'beyond the Pale' in Ireland, as George Orwell noted in his essays on his miserable experiences at his public school, is to create those who will administer it.

The first thing that must be brutalised is the subjectivity of those the colony seeks to privilege: they must be taught, violently if necessary, who is considered human and who is not, who is their own kind and who is not (our own kin, who are permitted kindness). They must be taught the price of treachery, the rewards of loyalty. They must be educated in the thousands and millions and billions of words that reinforce this in every sentence, every image, every map; the histories, the literatures, the libraries of propaganda. They must be rebuked, caned, punished, beaten, penalised, until the hierarchies of family, school, and university translate into the hierarchies of the empire, as natural and good as the empire itself. We bow down before the monster, and in return the monster gives us rights to everything: stories in which we are the heroes, a licence that says that, no matter how miserable and mean we are in the machinery of empire, we are still gods compared to those we have permission to brutalise and rob.

The colony must first be built at home, and then its nightmare can be exported for the good of the empire.

I said I would not feel guilty, because guilt is worse than useless, because guilt is one of the major weapons with which the empire builds itself. Guilt is the whip that ensures conformity and complicity. It paralyses action and poisons anger. It's the secret seed that flowers into the colonist's hatred and fear. But sometimes I do feel the point of shame.

Such a project in totalisation has constant glitches in the matrix: a flicker of humanity, a sudden moment of sadness, a flash of compassion that shows that perhaps the categories of humanness are not as taught. Often in Anglo culture, these moments are deflected onto animals: this conditioning goes so deep it can brutalise every relationship with another human being.

Orwell is one of the more perceptive writers about the subjectivity of the officials of empire, and unusually honest in how he articulates it. But he still fails to see the people he administers — or, not uncoincidentally, women — as fully human. In his famous essay 'Shooting an Elephant', he discusses the time when he was a sub-divisional police officer in Moulmein, Burma, when an elephant in must went rogue. He was already upset by his role as a hated oppressor:

> With one part of my mind I thought of the British Raj as an unbreakable tyranny, as something clamped down, in saecula saeculorum, upon the will of prostrate peoples; with another part I thought that the greatest joy in the world would be to drive a bayonet into a Buddhist priest's guts. Feelings like these are the normal by-products of imperialism.

The incident with the elephant, he says, enlightened him on 'the real nature of imperialism — the real motives for which despotic governments act'. It turns out that his central insight is that the empire's subjugated people, whom he mainly mentions with dislike, because of the hostility he encounters as he goes about his business, are actually responsible for the empire's violence:

> Here was I, the white man with his gun, standing in front of the unarmed native crowd — seemingly the leading actor of the piece; but in reality I was only an absurd puppet pushed to and fro by the will of those yellow faces behind.

I perceived in this moment that when the white man turns tyrant it is his own freedom that he destroys. He becomes a sort of hollow, posing dummy, the conventionalized figure of a sahib.

There's quite a bit to unpack here: there's a double movement that recognises the white man's tyranny, which in the same motion is deprived of agency. It's not the white man who acts with violence, but the crowd that surrounds him.

It's striking how Orwell portrays the British Empire itself as somehow free of agency: it's a series of actions that move like fate, independently of the people who administer it. On the one hand, he sees the 'dirty work of Empire at close quarters' very clearly: 'The wretched prisoners huddling in the stinking cages of the lock-ups, the grey, cowed faces of the long-term convicts, the scarred buttocks of the men who had been flogged with bamboos — all these oppressed me with an intolerable sense of guilt.' On the other hand, he could 'get nothing into perspective': 'I was young and ill-educated and I had had to think out my problems in the utter silence that is imposed on every Englishman in the East.' He hated what he did, but that didn't mean that he had any empathy for those whom the empire oppressed.

Orwell describes with a cold exactitude the horrific injuries of the man the elephant killed, the expression on his face of 'unendurable agony', his skin stripped from his back 'as neatly as one skins a rabbit'. Like the crowd that cheers when he shoots the elephant, the dead face is 'devilish'. The Burmese are described as a mob of yellow faces. The empathy he feels, when it is not towards himself as unjustly victimised by Buddhist monks, is entirely directed to the elephant he must kill: he spends paragraphs on its agonising death. He displaces his guilt by saying that he was forced to kill it by the Burmese; he is mainly relieved that the elephant killed a man because it put him legally in the right.

'I often wondered,' he says of the aftermath of shooting the elephant, 'whether any of the others grasped that I had done it solely to avoid looking a fool.' The ridicule of the subjugated is the worst thing that can happen to the tyrant. I can't but think of this, from Margaret Atwood's *Second Words*, which has morphed into a popular internet meme:

> 'Why do men feel threatened by women?' I asked a male friend of mine … 'I mean,' I said, 'men are bigger, most of the time, they can run faster, strangle better, and they have on the average a lot more money and power.' 'They're afraid women will laugh at them,' he said. 'Undercut their world view.' Then I asked some women students in a quickie poetry seminar I was giving, 'Why do women feel threatened by men?' 'They're afraid of being killed,' they said.

Orwell's account of shooting the elephant gives me the same conflicted feeling as when I read his essay 'Antisemitism in Britain': his honesty is admirable, because it exposes what otherwise remains hidden, but on the other hand the spectacle is distasteful. He remains anti-Semitic, although he feels it's unjust; he is unable to undo his reflexive prejudice. You can trace its effects all through his writing, just as you can trace his sexism. He knows that anti-Semitism is 'irrational', but he wasn't even aware of his sexism; he loathed the empire, but continued to believe, as he says in that essay, that 'English people are almost invariably gentle and law-abiding'.

Naturally, I can't help wondering if I am creating the same kind of spectacle as Orwell. I'm making a spectacle of my self. I see it through the only spectacles I possess. I squint, trying to perceive clearly, but there is so much that is beyond my perception. Like Orwell, I can't see what I can't see.

Orwell maintains his innocence: he is the unwitting cog in a machine he loathes. For all that he hates the empire, he wholly believes that the British Empire was 'a great deal better than the empires that are going to supplant it'. I look at Britain's histories of massacres, famines, economic violence, and sheer robbery. I wonder what he means by 'worse'.

As a child, I was horrified by the excesses of eighteenth-century Belgian colonials in the Congo, believing, as I had been taught, that the British were better than that (the colonial wittering you see at all levels of discourse, from illiterate abuse on Twitter to tomes of imperial history). But all that ignorance is carefully curated to preserve the amour-propre of the inner empire, the empire that is constructed in our consciousnesses from the moment we're born into it. It's not hard to find its atrocities: what's astonishing is how they somehow never become more than temporary glitches in the ongoing assumption of imperial goodness. All the atrocities are unfortunate exceptions.

You don't have to go as far back as Clive of India to find

the casual idioms of genocide. There's the 1943 Bengal famine, during which four million people died because Winston
Churchill ordered that food supplies be diverted from Bengal
to war efforts in Europe. I didn't know anything about, say,
the equally shocking brutalities that occurred during the
suppression of the Mau Mau revolt in 1950s Kenya. Professor
Caroline Elkins' book *Britain's Gulag: the brutal end of empire
in Kenya* details the imprisonment in concentration camps
of a million and a half people, of which tens of thousands,
possibly hundreds of thousands, of people died of beatings,
malnutrition, and disease. Tortures under interrogation were
sadistic beyond belief. No British official or civilian has been
prosecuted for these atrocities: most of the documents detailing them were destroyed. The inexplicable gaps in the usually
meticulous records was what prompted Elkins into her ten
years of research.

She originally bought the British story about its innate
innocence. 'When I presented my dissertation proposal to my
department in the winter of 1997,' she says, 'I was intending to
write a history of the success of Britain's civilizing mission in
the detention camps of Kenya.'

There are the massacre sites that dot the map of Australia,
the enslavement of Aboriginal Australians that was legally
sanctioned by state law until the 1970s. The ongoing erasures
of Indigenous culture and land that continue up to the present
day, many under the rubric of social and economic prudence.
Communities shut down because the government says it
'can't afford' the services to keep them going. The open-cut
mines that wound the country, the tailing dams full of poison,

suppurating wounds poisoning the pure reservoirs of water that have always been the saviour of this arid land.

And still we think we're innocent.

It's a long, dark road, labouring through the thickets of imperial fantasy.

The real nightmare is how the harm is reproduced, generation after generation, how profoundly flexible these delusions are, how they perpetuate their own oblivion. I see every day how the languages of social justice are appropriated by people who have only benefited from the structures that ensure their privilege: the paranoia that feeds the fantasies of white genocide; the wealthy, high-status men who push their agendas of 'reverse sexism'; the transphobic women who use their own sexed wounds to visit on others what has been done to them. The habits of erasure and brutalisation reach down into the very core of colonial consciousness, wounding us so that we might wound others, viciously refusing the insights that might free us all from these long-ingrained habits of abuse.

I see how that pattern is reproduced in my family, how the binaries of patriarchal norms have divided us, how colonialism's brutalisations have played out between us as vicious competition, emptying out any possibility of truth in order to defend the empty shell of a brutalised self. I see how these patterns are alienated and reproduced in miniature, how they have become intransigent, how they replicate the wounding over and over again.

All my life, I have struggled to free myself from these pat-terns. The damage that repeats, that refuses to acknowledge itself, that turns outward and inward, destroying possibilities in ourselves, in others. The corrosion between us.

I can't see how it can be undone. All that is left is refusal.

Long-since groundless ladders

Fact can be made to mean so many things, and meaning is where we all founder. On the other hand, I hold reason very dear. Reason is where I begin to weave meaning.

'Reason,' says Gillian Rose in *Love's Work*, 'is forever without ground.' Reason is a play of thought that we mistake for authority. When I think of reason, I think of Rilke's lovers:

> their bold
> high figures of heartplay,
> their towers of pleasure, their
> long-since groundless ladders, leaning
> on only each other, tremulously, —

Reason, like love, begins arbitrarily. We begin with one thought, which we connect to another, and then another, in patterns and movements which we consider to be rational. It begins with 'Let a equal x.'

When I studied algebra at school, I found this arbitrariness disconcerting; part of me wondered if this was allowed. It took my breath away.

I felt as if there ought to be some objective value of a, some kind of grounding measurement that meant that when you said a equals x, it meant something in the material world, that somewhere in the universe there had to be a's and x's that knew exactly what they were and that each meant a single thing, a unit of value that was more than a symbolic pawn in a game of logic. Why should a equal x? What arcane power do we hold that can simply determine that it does?

Perhaps I am simply comfortable with the ambiguities of language, and find the abstractions of mathematics discomforting. I have always had the capacity to exist in 'uncertainties, mysteries, doubts, without any irritable reaching after fact and reason'. Suspension in uncertainty has, I think (I cannot be sure), never caused me as much discomfort as it seems to cause many others. I have sometimes wondered if this means that there is something wrong with me.

I know that words are crude and full of ambiguity, like the tongues and lips and breath that say them, like the fingers that write them, like the bodies that absorb them. The world of numbers holds a different kind of sensual quality, one I imagine to be like certain kinds of music that you listen to as if they were disembodied.

What if where we began was wrong, and a and x are not equal at all?

Fact has become something of a sacred object, especially in this era of instant disinformation: it is like the smallest possible unit of certainty. If something is a fact, it follows that it is true. (Is that true? Can there be an untrue fact?) But how do we establish a fact? Each fact, which we assert with such confidence, such touching belief in certainty, generates its meanings from a web of relationship and context. It's raining in Melbourne! The drought isn't real! But five hundred kilometres away, cattle mumble at hay thrown onto bare dirt paddocks.

Sometimes the internet feels like an actualisation of the collective mind of humanity. Scrolling through Twitter can be like descending into an endless abyss: jostling together in a list directed by invisible algorithms are truths, lies, half-truths, half-lies, partial observations torn out of context and made to represent a whole and complex reality, simplifications, misunderstandings, deliberate deceptions, devastating insights, jokes, half-heard conversations, analyses both sober and intoxicated, automated messages, propaganda bots, pleas for help or sympathy, myths asserted as fact, facts asserted as myths, atrocities, games, people meeting, people being kind or cruel or thoughtless or thoughtful, friendships, generosities, profound thoughts, poems, paintings, works of art. Glimpses, glimpses, glimpses.

Dread, almost always. Almost always, there is an underlying feeling of barely controlled panic. Sometimes reading Twitter feels like a form of psychosis, live footage of global breakdown. Sometimes it feels like the opposite of that.

How do any of us cope with all this simultaneity?

—

Once I believed in language, for all its murk and ambiguity. If I could make my words clear enough, I thought, if I made them strong enough, truthful enough, careful enough, eventually we could discern each other's realities.

I no longer believe this. It isn't enough to speak, because communication exists in two actions: speaking and listening. It doesn't matter how clear my words are, if the other isn't listening. Even with clarity, we fall into the jagged gulfs of misunderstanding. We wander into the dark forest and find no Virgil. We become trapped in the snare. We lose ourselves in our metaphors, and they become more real than whatever it is that we want to say.

And yet ... it's not entirely true that I have lost faith. If I had, I wouldn't be writing this. It's more that my faith has become qualified. To the best of my knowledge, I'm being truthful when I say that I have given up any hope of communicating with my sister. Am I nevertheless writing this to her, in the hope that perhaps, beyond hope, there exists the possibility of some other understanding? No. Yes. No.

I don't know.

I no longer know who I am. All my memories are suspect, shot through with a dark light. I guess I'm writing this primarily to myself, to memories that I now think I misunderstood. I am attempting to understand my own complicities. I am writing to that absence in myself.

I am trying to name an absence, at least. Not the obvious absence, I think, but something more complicated.

—

Alice Walker once wrote: 'Work is love made visible.' I read this when I was sinking beneath the new burden of motherhood, sleepless for three months with a colicky baby, not knowing what my life would be, realising that I had never known what my life would be, that I had never known who I was. The labour of looking after this new baby, the crushing exhaustion, the almost madness, opened into the purest love I have ever known.

There is nothing easy about love. And yet also it is all ease, all the permeability of need that swings now this way, now that way. I know that love makes it possible to work past brokenness, that the broken thing can be more beautiful because of the time and care that it took to put everything back together again. I know this because it has happened to me. Because we all made it happen, when our family was broken, when it seemed that everything had been lost. My children, my husband, me, we all bear the scars of that time, they are part of who we are. Out of the rubble that was all that was left all those many years ago, after violence and trauma and terrible betrayal, we built a trust that is a living thing, a trust that we tend together. And yes, that trust may at any time be broken. Because we know that, we are careful. We call each other up, we ask how the others are, we are indignant when one of us is hurting, we worry. We count our blessings and wonder when our luck will run out.

My daughter shows me a photo of herself. There she is, wearing the ancient charm against the evil eye, the blue and white μάτι painted on her nails, a pendant on her breast. Defiant, beautiful. I catch my breath at her Greek beauty, a beauty that is hers and not from me, the glossy hair and cheekbones and skin that come from her Greek father, who has never deserved her, and her grandmother, whom she loved and deserved to know better than she did.

'In magical circles,' I read on the internet, 'the evil eye falls under the category of "invisible" assault, a method of directing an envious or mean-spirited will against another. This is the worst kind of behaviour, as it involves covertly destroying the character, reputation, and overall well-being of someone else. Just like love (traditionally thought of as the most powerful form of magic), hatred is an infectious and tangible force that can create a whole host of psychological and physical disturbances.' The evil eye is cast by jealousy of another's good fortune. 'It is commonly believed,' I read on Wikipedia, 'that the evil eye can be given in the guise of a compliment, signifying its connection to the destructive power of jealousy.'

You can curse yourself, simply by acting without humility and inviting misfortune. This is perhaps why I do not want to write about the things that are precious in my life: out of fear that by naming them, they will be coveted and damaged, out of that ancient fear that by making my blessings visible, I may lose them. I know the power of the malignant eye. And this, after all, is the time of plague and war, when no one is safe, when the wind is full of invisible maladies.

Avert, the spell says.

Power of wind have I over thee.
Power of wrath have I over thee.
Power of fire have I over thee …

I first read this incantation as a child in Alan Garner's story *The Moon of Gomrath*. (Why did I want to be a poet? Because writing poems is a form of magic.) Garner used real spells in his stories, but he said he put only part of them in, just in case. He would have found this particular spell in Volume II of the *Carmina Gadelica: hymns and incantations, with illustrative notes on words, rites, and customs, dying and obsolete, orally collected in the Highlands and Islands of Scotland* by Alexander Carmichael. Garner didn't merely shorten the poem; as all writers do, he changed it for his own purposes. In *The Moon of Gomrath*, the spell is used against a brollachan, a malignant shadow that possesses the bodies of others, an entity that in Gaelic folklore is originally a malevolent water spirit.

The original spell wards against the evil eye.

Garner's version addresses *thee*. But the original, as translated from Gaelic by Carmichael, addresses the curse: the *it*.

And me, I do not want power over thee. I want power over the curse that has warped my life. Not thee. *It*.

I spend hours trying to find out what the word 'iuc' means in the incantation. A meadow? A mountain? An expanse? Is it a particularly untranslatable kind of cow paddock? I search dictionaries of Gaelic, but no dice. Why did Carmichael not translate it? Is it a typo?

But perhaps instead I should be thinking about the 'Three of Life' in the final stanza, the 'Sacred Three', the 'Secret Ones'. They are masquerading here as the Holy Trinity, the Father, the Son, and the Holy Ghost, but that's a Christian mask over ancient resonances. The Secret Ones are the triple-headed moon goddess. Hecate, Persephone, Selene. 'Triple-sounding, triple-headed, triple-voiced, triple-pointed, triple-faced, triple-necked.' The three Charites, the three Moirai, the three Erinyes. The three sisters. Grace, Fate, and Retribution.

I say the poem to myself over again:

I trample upon the eye,
As tramples the duck upon the lake,
As tramples the swan upon the water,
As tramples the horse upon the place,
As tramples the cow upon the iuc,
As tramples the host of the elements,
    As tramples the host of the elements.

Power of wind I have over it,
Power of wrath I have over it,
Power of fire I have over it,
Power of thunder I have over it,
Power of lightning I have over it,
Power of storms I have over it,
Power of moon I have over it,
Power of sun I have over it,
Power of stars I have over it,
Power of firmament I have over it,
Power of the heavens
And of the worlds I have over it,
    Power of the heavens
    And the world I have over it.

A portion of it upon the grey stones,
A portion of it upon the steep hills,
A portion of it upon the fair meads,
And a portion upon the great salt sea,
She herself is the best instrument to carry it,

    The great salt sea,

    The best instrument to carry it.

In name of the Three of Life,
In name of the Sacred Three,
In name of all the Secret Ones,

    And of the Powers together.

A beginning, maybe

I listen to Antony and the Johnsons' 'You Are My Sister'. It's always been a song that reaches into my chest and tears out my heart. For the first time, I allow my sorrow to rise to the surface.

I sit at my desk and let myself weep. Unbitter tears, without hope or expectation.

Beyond the words, the wound of Anohni's voice, its winding, throbbing beauty that pierces the armour of language into the truth. The truth is grief. Underneath everything is grief. It's grief for the person I might have been, for the person she might have been, for what we have lost, together and alone, for what is irrevocable, for what I know is no longer possible.

Yes, there is a freedom, but it comes at a price. It puts me beyond the pale, where I will never be fully at home, where perhaps, all the same, I can make a home.

Forgiveness isn't something I can do on my own. We

will never find a ground that isn't riven and salted by these damaged histories.

I used to think love was enough, but it isn't. Perhaps the single thing I have learned over my five decades walking on this planet is that love is only the beginning. It's the seed that makes everything else possible, but it can grow crooked, it can be thwarted and broken and stunted. It can be turned into a prison, an instrument of torture. Its lack can poison the air and the ground.

We begin to love with the small things. If we are lucky. We begin with ourselves, with the people we touch, the breasts of our mother, those things that we know as home, as part of us. If we're lucky, if we're safe, we grow. We learn to think outside our own skins; we learn, painfully, joyfully, to take off the blinkers that hide us from the world, that hide the world from us.

But that process is so fragile, and the world is full of weapons.

There is no condition of my sister's safety in which I am not destroyed. There is no expiation that doesn't begin with the same lie that poisons us both. I can't be her monster anymore, and I can't anymore be the angel who accepts my monstrousness to enable her self-love. I can't creep through this dark labyrinth looking for a truth that isn't there.

I don't know what determines why one person goes this way and another that. We make choices, and choices cascade from those choices, and suddenly we find ourselves in a strange country where a keen, cold wind is blowing away everything that we thought we knew.

I began with the anguish of rage. I am left holding this love, which now can only be pain. For my own sake, I have to learn to admit this love and know it for what it is, without bitterness, without hope, without possibility.

It is what it is. Nothing more.

Nothing less.

Acknowledgements

Some passages in this book have been repurposed from columns that were first published in *Overland* literary journal.

I would like to thank the many, many people besides those named in the book whose writings, insights, and courage have helped my thinking and writing. Thanks too to Marika Webb-Pullman for commissioning *Monsters*, and to David Golding, who has been the insightful, meticulous editor I needed to guide me through these bewildering thickets. Lastly, and always, love to family: my children, Josh, Zoe, and Ben, and my husband, Daniel. Thank you for everything.